CBI SERIES IN MANAGEMENT COMMUNICATIONS

Writing the Business and Technical Report

CBI SERIES IN MANAGEMENT COMMUNICATIONS

William J. Gallagher, Series Editor
Arthur D. Little, Inc.

Mastering the Business and Technical Presentation
Leonard F. Meuse, Jr.

Developing Reading Skills for Business and Industry
Richard P. Santeusanio

Writing the Business and Technical Report
William J. Gallagher

Listen! A Skill Guide for Business and Industry
Thomas E. Anastasi

The Manager as an Editor
Louis Visco

Writing the Business and Technical Report

William J. Gallagher

CBI PUBLISHING COMPANY, INC.
51 Sleeper Street
Boston, Massachusetts 02210

Production Editor: Deborah Flynn
Text Designer: Roy Howard Brown
Compositor: Modern Graphics
Cover Designer: Betsy Franklin

Library of Congress Cataloging in Publication Data

Gallagher, William J
    Writing the business and technical report.

    (CBI series in management communications)
    1. Business report writing—Problems,
exercises, etc.   2. Technical writing—Problems,
exercises, etc.   I. Title.   II. Series.
HF5719.G34   808'.066651021   80-19781
ISBN 0-8436-0796-3

Printed in the United States of America

Printing (*last digit*): 9 8 7 6 5 4 3 2 1

In Memory of Robert

The measure of achievement is
not how long one lives
but how well.

Contents

Editor's Foreword   ix
Preface   xi

1. Preliminary Considerations: The Who's and the Why's   1

2. Organization: Focus and Impact   7

3. Outlining: Building the Framework   31

4. Preparing the Draft: Points About Procedure   42

5. Orderly Development: The Paragraph Principle   46

6. Editing the Draft: Applying the Finish   70

7. Using Tables and Illustrations   105

Appendix I Conventions   129
Appendix II Answers to Exercises   141

Editor's Foreword

Despite the magnitude and acceleration of change during the past two decades, the functions of management remain essentially the same: to make decisions, to plan, to organize, to get things done, and to measure the results. Before decisions can be made, however, information must be transferred. Before tasks can be accomplished, behavior may have to be modified. And communication is still the only means we have to reach these objectives.

The basic problem with communication stems from how we view the process. The first image the term evokes is usually of someone speaking or writing. Implicit in this image, of course, is that this activity is directed at someone else in the background. But the emphasis is on the transmitter rather than on the receiver. According to this perception, communication is always one-directional.

This perception assumes that to communicate, all we need to do is talk or write. The corollaries of this assumption are that the message intended is always conveyed and that logic and clarity are enough to guarantee persuasion. Consequently, a great deal of the training in oral and written communication has been oriented toward the speaker or writer. Guidelines for the listener or reader are usually ignored.

This text is one of a series based on the premise that no one merely communicates. Rather, he or she communicates something to someone. And that someone—the listener or reader—is very important. He or she is not, as many apparently believe, a passive element receiving information without coloring or response. On the contrary, the receiver is continually reacting to the expression of ideas in light of personal experience, interests, and values. Therefore, in any communication the receiver adds their own dimension to the meaning and then responds to what he or she has added. Communication is thus interactive, and being interactive, it requires the cooperation of sender and receiver.

Effective communication ensures cooperation by anticipation and adaptation. It considers the communication objective, the subject, and the audience. It recognizes the environment in which the communication is to take place, the external and internal factors that affect it, and the extent of the control needed by both sender and receiver to neutralize these factors. It recognizes that selecting the appropriate medium is as important as tailoring the presentation.

This communication series was prepared in recognition of the fact that the receiver is the most important element in communication, for he or she is not only the reason for the communication but the measure by which its success is evaluated. In the texts designed to help the sender, the guidelines are aimed at improving skills by anticipating problems posed by the receiver. In the texts designed for the receiver, the guidelines are aimed at improving the ability to assimilate information by cooperating with the sender.

The authors of the CBI Series in Management Communications have a distinctive combination of skills as practitioners and teachers. Each is employed by an organization that places heavy emphasis on communication. Each has also spent many years in teaching communication through formal academic courses and through seminars sponsored by government and industry. Collectively, they possess diverse experience in industry, government, and education.

The texts therefore address the needs of business and government and the various circumstances in which these needs for communication skills are evident. Each of the authors is aware of these needs not only because of his position, but because of the numerous opportunities he has had to discuss them with others at various levels of management. The guidelines presented, therefore, offer a realistic and practical approach to effective communication.

The texts can be used as guides for self-training or as the basis for formal group training in college classes or in seminars sponsored by government and industry. Although written independently with only broad guidelines and coordination by the editor, they have a unity of purpose and design. The books can therefore be used collectively by those interested in the broad spectrum of communication or individually by those with selected interests.

Since all of the authors are realists, we do not offer guidelines as magic potions guaranteeing instantaneous success. Principles and techniques do not ensure success. Motivation and a great deal of effort are also required. Our objective is to show you the way; the goal is yours to attain.

William J. Gallagher, Editor
CBI Series in Management Communications

Preface

Truman Capote's riposte about the prose of a well-known writer aptly describes many business and technical reports: "That's not writing. That's typing!" Some reports are ineffective because the people who prepare them look on writing as a necessary evil. Their real objective therefore is not to communicate carefully but to dispense with the task quickly. Other reports are ineffective because the people who prepare them never learned to write. While in school, they considered writing courses to be not very functional—designed more for dilettantes than for engineers, scientists, and businessmen.

This book is designed not to lessen the time you spend on report writing, but to help you use that time more effectively. It will have served its purpose if it provides fresh insights as it re-acquaints you with some principles and techniques that you may have either ignored or misunderstood. It offers no magic formula, only fundamentals and a common-sense approach. I hope, however, that along the way you will discover a few suggestions that will make report writing more satisfying.

No one writes a book without help. I received help from various quarters: those who contributed samples, those who offered suggestions, those who reviewed the manuscript. I am especially grateful to my son Bill, who prepared several of the illustrations in Chapter 7, and to my secretary, Catherine Harvey, who typed the manuscript and incorporated my numerous revisions in an endless display of patience and fortitude.

WJG
Lowell, MA

1
Preliminary Considerations: The Who's and the Why's

If you are like most people who have to write reports, you probably follow a two-step procedure. The first step is to delay writing and hope that the person who requested the report will decide eventually that he or she does not need it. The second step is to recognize reality and to begin writing according to the "magic rectangle" method.

The principle of the "magic rectangle" is simple. Paragraphs are viewed as rectangles whose dimensions are fixed by the writer. The report, therefore, becomes a series of rectangles whose areas are filled by thoughts as they occur to the writer. Thus, the first thought that comes to mind becomes sentence one of paragraph one; the second thought becomes sentence two of paragraph one; the third becomes sentence three of paragraph one; and the process continues until the writer happens to glance at his paper and thinks, "Gee, it's been a good while since I indented." At that point, the next thought that occurs to him becomes the first sentence of paragraph two!

As you can see, this procedure requires very little effort of the writer. Each paragraph becomes a receptacle that accepts spill-over from a previous paragraph. Structure is of little or no concern since physical dimension is the only consideration.

To the reader, of course, the effort is considerable. Because the report lacks focus and direction, because the individual paragraphs are not developed around single ideas, and because the ideas do not progress clearly and logically, the reader often has to attempt to reconstruct the report before he can understand it. And since most readers are not willing to expend this kind of effort, many reports go unread or undigested.

No one wants to write reports that go unread or unappreciated. Since even careless writing requires some investment of time and effort, the extra effort required to ensure that your report will be read and assimilated is time well spent. Therefore, the next time you have to write a report, give some thought to it before you pick up a pencil to write.

ESTABLISH YOUR OBJECTIVE

Your first consideration should be: "Why am I writing this report?" Your answer, however, should not be merely: "Because so-and-so asked me to." Although this kind of answer may establish responsiveness, dependability, or just resignation, it does not establish what the report should accomplish.

In general, reports are designed to inform or to persuade. Typical of those designed to inform are progress reports, explanations of policies and procedures, and various kinds of analyses. Typical of those designed to persuade are reports that propose a course of action, recommend one of several options, or support a position.

Writers usually do not have a problem establishing their objective when the report falls unmistakably into one of these two categories. If, for example, you were asked to bring your boss up to date on a project on which you were working, your objective would be clearly to inform. Similarly, if you wrote a report justifying a request for additional space or staff, the intent would be clearly to persuade.

Establishing the objective usually becomes a problem when neither the subject of the report nor the request for it defines the intent. For example, suppose you are asked to prepare a report that discusses a revised benefits and compensation package. The objective could be merely to acquaint employees with the revisions or it could be to assure them that the revised package is better than the original. Therefore, when a report is solicited, make sure that you and the person requesting it agree on what it is intended to accomplish.

When a report is unsolicited, of course, the full responsibility for establishing the objective rests with the writer. Sometimes even though a writer states a purpose or objective in a report, it may not be the principal purpose. For example, he may write: "This report discusses the need for training back-up operators." The unstated but more important objective, however, may be to obtain approval of additional funding for training when stringent economic measures are being adopted throughout the company. Sometimes, therefore, playing down the real objective may be a deliberate strategy. At other times, however, it may be neglected simply because the writer failed to perceive its importance. In such instances, the focus of the report and hence the selection and arrangement of detail are affected.

Whether you state your objective explicitly in the report or not, be sure at least to take the time to determine what it is before you start to prepare the report. Defining your objective will help you to decide whether it is achievable in view of the scope of the material you plan to present and of the authority, interests, and attitude of the reader(s).

CONSIDER YOUR READER(S)

Unlike novelists, playwrights, and journalists, report writers usually address a highly select and definable audience. Most readers of reports have fairly narrow technical, economic, or professional interests and directly related needs. To make certain that your report gets its message across most effectively, therefore, consider three basic questions as part of a reader profile.

What Information Is Needed?

To determine the reader's needs, it is helpful to know how he plans to use the report and what his interests and responsibilities are.

Determining how the reader plans to use the report involves whether he needs the information only for himself or whether he intends to disseminate the information to others. If he plans on using the information himself, does he need it as a basis for decision or merely to expand his knowledge of a subject or a procedure? If he intends to disseminate the information, does he plan on distributing your report intact or on extracting key ideas for incorporation in another report?

Knowing his interests and responsibilities will help you to determine the relative importance of types of information. For example, a research director, production manager, and sales director might all be interested in the feasibility of introducing a new plastic product, but from different points of view. The research director would be interested primarily in the scientific and technical aspects; the production manager, in equipment; and the sales director, in markets and distribution. In a report to the research director, therefore, formulations, experimental methods, and theory might be of principal importance; the design and operation of production equipment might be of secondary importance; and distribution methods might be of no importance.

Determining the reader's need for information is often a matter of determining the scope of the report. Because of a misunderstanding about what considerations should be included in a discussion, readers often accuse report writers of not providing enough information or of providing needless information. Therefore, if you are not sure of all the areas that should be covered, do not guess or assume. Find out. It's worth the extra time.

Sometimes you can find out merely by asking. Sometimes, however, you cannot, especially if the subject is highly technical or highly complex, or if the person requesting the information is a generalist rather than a specialist. In such instances, you may have to help him by suggesting considerations based on your experience and by allowing him to revise your suggested scope on the basis of his perceived needs.

In any event, defining the scope and agreeing on it will not only prevent misconceptions between writer and reader and allow you to collect information more efficiently, but will also provide a firmer base for the findings, conclusions, and/or recommendations advanced in the report.

What Is His Knowledge of the Subject?

Depending on such variables as education, experience, and position, readers can be classified as well informed, generally informed, or uninformed. The well-informed reader is usually a specialist with extensive training and experience. The generally informed reader is usually one who has had some training and experience in the area but who has become involved more with administration and management than with technology and procedure. The uninformed reader is usually one who has had little or no need, opportunity, or incentive to become familiar with the subject. For example, to explain the advantages of computerizing billing, payroll, and other financial functions, it may be necessary for a financially oriented manager to become acquainted with some of the technology and programming associated with computers.

To make sure your reader understands the issues and ideas you plan to present, therefore, make sure that the amount and discussion of information you include is commensurate with his background and familiarity with the subject. Underestimating the reader's knowledge can lead you to include unnecessary explanation and detail, whereas overestimating his knowledge of the subject can lead to omission of detail necessary to his understanding. In the first case, you may be accused of being condescending; in the second, you may be accused of being inconsiderate or arrogant.

What Is His Attitude?

Many people act as though attitude is a permanent part of a person, like an arm or a leg. Whether we define it in aeronautical or in psychological terms, however, *attitude* is our position in relation to something else. Since the position we assume affects how we perceive things, whenever we change position we alter our perception and also our attitude.

Depending on their attitude, readers are either favorably disposed toward the writer's position, unfavorably disposed toward it, or neutral.

The reader who is favorably disposed toward the writer's position poses little or no problem because he can be counted on to support the writer's view or at least to be amenable to it. Because he operates at the same level, or under the same pressures, or in the same environment, he usually perceives things much the same way as the writer does. Therefore, there is little need to dwell on points the reader readily accepts. All that is needed is to maintain his interest.

The reader who is unfavorably disposed toward the writer's point of view may have adopted this attitude because he has substituted emotion for knowledge, distorted information that seemed threatening to him, or accepted only those ideas that he understands and rejected those he does not understand. The effective writer recognizes that this type of reader cannot be communicated with beyond his power to comprehend or beyond the consequences he perceives for himself. In dealing with hostility, therefore, the writer must recognize that he cannot force a change of opinion. All he can hope for is to develop respect for his point of view by providing comprehensive review, by pointing out areas of agreement, and by explaining how he reached his point of view.

The neutral reader has no preconceptions. He is willing to allow his thinking to be influenced by the weight of the evidence. This type of reader, however, recognizes bias and often plays the devil's advocate. Consequently, if the writer slants information, confuses fact and opinion or fact and assumption, or in any way fails to discuss the issues objectively, the neutral reader may be influenced to take an opposing point of view.

TAILOR THE INFORMATION

Because you address a report to someone is no guarantee that it will be read promptly, completely, and carefully. Your report competes for the reader's time not only with other reports but also with a great many other things that require his attention. Therefore, whether your report is read, when it is read, and how well it is read depend on the reader's perception of its value.

In one respect, therefore, every report you write is a sales document regardless of the subject. You are selling the usefulness of information or of an idea, an evaluation, a method, or a recommendation. Like any product that seeks to win support or approval, reports require craftsmanship.

Tailoring the report recognizes the reader's priorities through a review of the profile of background, interests, needs, convictions, and environment developed by analysis. It then adapts substance, structure, and style to meet the communication objective. In short, it introduces the right kind of information at the right time in the right amounts in language that is clear and compelling. In so doing, it anticipates questions and biases, provides reasons, distinguishes between fact and assumption, and draws on the familiar to explain the unfamiliar.

Tailoring considers both the emotional and the rational aspects of communication. It is not enough to write something that can be read. Effective communication depends on the extent to which the words represent the same thing for the reader as they do for the writer. Emotional responses are affected by the tone that words convey and by the way that topics are introduced. The careful writer is neither condescending nor arrogant. While making the reader feel knowledgeable and intelligent, he suggests that the reader may have overlooked certain points or that certain information may not have been available to him before. There is a difference between preaching and merely calling attention to something. People appreciate suggestions on how to do things faster, better, or more economically, but they do not like to be dictated to.

In summary, remember that the reader is not only the reason the report was written, but is also the measure by which its success is judged. The decision to support or approve the ideas advanced in the report rests with him. Therefore, concentrate on the reader and accommodate the subject to him.

2
Organization: Focus and Impact

THE NEED FOR DESIGN

Anyone who has taken an aptitude test is probably familiar with diagnostics. One such method of testing involves examining a series of digits and supplying an omitted digit in the series. For example, you might be asked to identify the missing digit in the following series:

3, 6, 12, 24, 48, 96, _____.

It is not difficult in this simple series to identify 192 as the missing digit, because it is apparent that each subsequent digit in the progression is a doubling of the previous one.

Suppose, however, that you were expected to identify 192 as the missing digit in the following series, which uses exactly the same digits used in the series above:

3, 96, 6, 48, 12, 24, _____.

You would probably find it extremely difficult, if not impossible, because the relationship between the digits is not immediately evident from the progression. For all practical purposes, the selection of digits appears to be random. In short, design aids understanding by providing a governing principle with which a series of facts conforms.

This underlying principle of design aids not only understanding but also memory. For example, if you were to listen to a recital of the digits in the first series above, you could undoubtedly recall them much more easily than the second because memory is aided by the perception of relationships or organizational pattern. When the design is not perceptible, we must multiply the effort required to understand and retain individual details; and while attempting to retain some, we often garble or lose others.

So it is with reports. Without design, concepts and factual detail lack cohesiveness. Regardless of how striking individual thoughts may be, they lose impact when they seem to have no focus or direction. Appropriate organization, therefore, is the key to effective communication because it provides focus, direction, and impact.

ESTABLISHING THE FOCUS

The focus of a report, and hence the appropriateness of the organizational pattern, is determined largely by the writer's objective and by the reader's needs and attitude toward the subject; this focus is expressed in the central idea. As a result, the central idea governs the selection and arrangement of detail. Any topic that does not relate to the central idea does not belong in the report. Each topic should be so arranged that the development of the central idea proceeds logically, easily, and persuasively.

Many writers assume that they provide a central idea when they merely write a broad statement of the subject to be covered. For example, "The purpose of this report is to discuss the financial status of XYZ Company" is not a statement of the central idea. A central idea is a more definitive statement—an observation, conclusion, recommendation, or opinion offered for consideration as a result of the writer's research, experience, or creative thinking. Thus, in a report discussing the financial condition of XYZ Company, the writer might establish as his central idea "XYZ Company is in the strongest financial position in its history" or "XYZ Company has weathered a difficult period and the outlook is promising."

The distinction between the subject of the report and the central idea is important. The central idea includes key terms that identify specific aspects of the subject on which the report is to focus, whereas a broad statement of the subject does not. For example, by stating that you are going to discuss the financial status of XYZ Company, you allow yourself a broad latitude of discussion, much of which may not impinge on the issues of greatest importance. Consequently, important points may be overlooked by inadequate development or clouded by irrelevant detail. By including key words and phrases, the central idea addresses specific issues and forms the foundation on which the report is constructed.

Here are some examples of central ideas. Note that they are complete sentences, which establish the relationships between key terms requiring development.

Subject	Central Idea
Office Space	Renovating existing space is less expensive than constructing additional facilities.
In-house Publication	Producing documents in-house normally provides greater control and economy than subcontracting does.
Electronic Funds-Transfer Systems	Electronic funds-transfer systems will require banks to take a new look at their markets and market strategies.
Television Programming	Television programming is influenced more by the Nielsen ratings than by the quality of the production.
Evaluation of PDQ Facility	The PDQ facility needs to upgrade its equipment and reduce waste if it is to remain competitive.

Where the central idea is expressed normally depends on whether the reader is decision-oriented or procedure-oriented. Management readers, for example, are generally more interested in results or suggested action than they are in method or analytical detail. To this kind of audience, therefore, the central idea may be stated as a finding, conclusion, or recommendation. In a long report, it is usually stated in the Summary, which precedes the detailed discussion. In a short report, it is stated at or near the beginning. To a procedure-oriented audience, it may be preferable to discuss the procedural details before stating the results.

The location of the central idea also depends on the anticipated response of the reader. If the writer believes that his central idea is controversial or that it may be unpalatable to the reader, he may choose to delay introducing it until he has dispensed with perceived barriers. Thus, for example, in recommending his choice of alternatives, he may delay stating his preference until he has discussed the disadvantages of others towards which he knows his reader is predisposed.

The important thing to remember, however, is that wherever you introduce the central idea, make sure it appears carefully considered and reasonable. Moreover, whether it is expressed or implied in a report, make certain that you write it out explicitly when preparing the report. The central idea governs the organization.

PATTERNS OF ORGANIZATION

Having established the central idea, you must support it. Facts seldom speak for themselves. Their significance grows out of their relationship. Hence, it is important to select the most appropriate structure.

The Chronological Pattern

In this pattern, events or facts are arranged in a step-by-step or time sequence. The chronological pattern is most useful when you are discussing the history of a subject, describing a process, recounting an itinerary, or explaining a procedure.

Suppose, for example, you have to discuss the evolution of a new product. You might find it useful to arrange your discussion in time-related stages.

Design

Development

Test and Evaluation

Production

Marketing

This pattern is commonly employed in progress reports. Because the project is being reviewed against a plan, it has a schedule and definable stages. Therefore, the report is normally arranged into activities or steps that have been completed, that are being worked on, and that remain to be worked on. The report thus places the project into a past-present-future context relating to the period covered.

It is especially useful when instruction or orientation is the principal objective. Manuals dealing with the installation, operation, and maintenance of equipment, for example, discuss the subjects in terms of a succession of necessary steps. So, too, in a report prepared to orient readers about a phototypesetting system, the writer might choose to discuss the components in the order in which they are used in the process.

Typewriter Input

Optical Character Recognition

The Central Processor

High-Speed Printer

Video Display Terminals

Photocomposer

Film Processor

The chronological pattern is also useful in detailing the steps followed in a test or experiment. In such instances, the writer's objective is to emphasize method or procedure. With this information, the reader may either duplicate the procedure if it achieved the desired results, or consider variations or a completely different approach if it did not.

Because it is a convenient and fairly simple way to organize information, the chronological pattern is used almost exclusively by many writers regardless of their objective. Obviously, however, this pattern is not always appropriate. When it isn't, the report may lose its effectiveness.

Consider, for example, this memorandum addressed to the Director of Marketing.

From: D. B. Jones

To: J. Peters

Subject: American Dental Association Convention

The purpose of this memorandum is to provide information gathered during two days spent at the American Dental Association national convention in Las Vegas.

A record attendance of more than 14,000 dentists was reported. With the exception of some delays at registration booths, the convention was extremely well managed and the exhibitor booths were attractively decorated.

The four-man professional sales force did an outstanding job. They volunteered to work continuously from 9 A.M. until 5 P.M. I am particularly impressed with Sam Steele, who appeared to be the leader of the group. He is extremely well informed, friendly, and persuasive.

The flashlight mirror, serving as a free premium with the purchase of three gallons of Product Y, was well received. This premium is ideal because it generated excitement among dentists and is directly connected to their practice.

A large percentage of the dentists complained that because of the size of the gallon bottle of Product Y, they didn't have room to store adequate supplies in their offices. As a result, many have switched to other brands. Of those who continue to use it, 70 percent dilute it; consequently, it is doubtful that patients, in many instances, recognize this weak solution as Product Y.

I believe there is a real opportunity to sell Product Y concentrate to dentists. A preliminary formula has already been developed by R&D. If it could be successfully marketed, it would significantly reduce Product Y shipping costs and help to solve the space problem.

Although Product Y is the company's major product and therefore of major concern to the Marketing Director, he might never become aware of the problem if he depended solely on that memo for information. Managers who receive many reports attempt frequently to establish the importance of the information contained in reports by glancing at the subject line and the first paragraph or two. On the basis of this skimming, they decide to read the report in its entirety, or put it aside until they attend to matters with higher priority, or file it without further reading. To the action-oriented reader, important considerations presented in chronological sequence may take too long to unfold. In the above memorandum, the subject line and the sequence of events emphasizes the convention rather than the problem.

If, as it appears, the problem is the most important consideration, it should have been identified after the statement of purpose. Furthermore, Product Y should have been identified in the subject line in conjunction with the convention. Finally, the report should be revised, either as a separate report dealing only with the problem or as a restructured report highlighting the problem and providing transitions that lead from the problem to the favorable aspects covered in the original report.

Topical Pattern
This method of organization is based on the inherent divisions of a subject. Sometimes they are broad considerations. For example, computers could be discussed in terms of hardware and software; budgets, in terms of receipts and expenditures; products, in terms of supply and demand; and investment strategies, in terms of advantages and disadvantages. Sometimes the divisions are more restrictive: requirements or criteria agreed on in advance by the writer and reader or limitations on the scope of the discussion imposed solely by the writer.

If, for example, in an evaluation of equipment the agreed on criteria were how easy it is to operate, how much downtime it could be expected to incur, how safe it is for operators, and how much it costs, then the topical arrangement would logically include these considerations:

Performance

Safety

Cost

On the other hand, in a report responding to a request for your reaction to a proposal to prepare a series of films on the operations of a bank for adult audiences in the community, the topical divisions would be an outgrowth of the number of observations included in your reaction.

Observations	Topics for Discussion
1. There have been few requests for such films during the past three years.	I. Demand
2. No one in our organization is available to handle the assignment.	II. Staff Availability
3. We do not have enough budget to have them produced by film-producing companies.	III. Budget Restrictions
4. Films such as the type you propose are available on request from other sources.	IV. Alternative Sources of Supply

The topical pattern is commonly used in analytical reports and in reports that define a problem and suggest a solution. As a result, it is usually based on a conclusion or a recommendation, which is developed by the discussion arranged by topic.

The topics are normally arranged according to their importance to and impact on the reader. Depending on how the writer anticipates the reader will react to the most important consideration, he may arrange the topics in ascending or descending order. If he feels the most important consideration will be viewed favorably, he may state it first and include the others in descending order of importance. If he feels the most important topic will be viewed unfavorably and thus bias the overall reaction, however, he may elect to arrange the topics in ascending order and discuss the least important ones first.

The flexibility of the pattern allows him to adapt it to the reader in much the same way that a salesman discusses a product. Suppose, for example, you walked into an automobile agency to inquire about a new car. Recognizing that price, the most important consideration to most customers, is usually a hurdle, the salesman normally discusses favorable features first: styling, safety, comfort, ease of handling, conveniences, and so forth. He hopes that these considerations, in the aggregate, will outweigh the price disadvantages and thus influence a favorable reaction. If, however, during a special three-day sale the price were so drastically reduced that it no longer posed a purchase barrier, the salesman would undoubtedly mention it first.

Many writers may feel that presenting information this way slants it and ignores objectivity. Not so. Objectivity requires that all relevant evidence be discussed, and this approach does discuss all the information. It merely places information strategically rather than omitting it. Moreover, the strategy is based on the conviction that the conclusion or recommendation is a truthful, complete, and valid assessment that will benefit the reader. In short, it is worth a persuasive effort, and the flexibility of the pattern is therefore used as an aid to persuasion.

Alternatives Pattern

The alternatives pattern discusses a number of possible options in terms of specific criteria. The development provides the rationale and documentation by which the unsuitable or less suitable options were eliminated and the most suitable was determined. It is often employed in reports dealing with such subjects as new-product opportunities, routes to diversification, and similar evaluations.

The alternatives pattern is essentially a modification of the topical pattern. The distinction between the two patterns is that in the topical, the discussion is arranged in terms of criteria, whereas in the alternatives, it is arranged in terms of possible options.

Suppose, for example, that you are asked to analyze three sites as potential locations for a management training center. The bases for the evaluation might be enough acreage for a campus atmosphere, accessibility to public transportation, and development costs. If the sites are to be emphasized in the discussion, as is normally the case, the alternatives pattern is best.

I. Site A
    Acreage

        Accessibility
        Development Costs
  II. Site B
        Acreage
        Accessibility
        Development Costs
  III. Site C
        Acreage
        Accessibility
        Development Costs

If for some reason, however, the criteria required emphasis, the topical pattern would be more appropriate.

  I. Acreage
        Site A
        Site B
        Site C
  II. Accessibility
        Site A
        Site B
        Site C
  III. Development Costs
        Site A
        Site B
        Site C

When several options are being considered, the alternatives pattern is best, because it provides a cohesive and complete overview of each option. By emphasizing criteria, and hence using the topical pattern, the discussion of options is fragmented and therefore requires that the reader synthesize the details relating to each option in order to develop the proper perspective.

Psychological-Progression Pattern

This pattern is similar to the alternatives pattern, in that it explores the value of several options. It differs, however, in intent and therefore in the scope of the options. Whereas the alternatives pattern is restricted to apparently logical and potentially appropriate options to determine the best, the psychological-progression pattern also includes illogical and inappropriate options in an attempt at nullifying reader biases, which are usually rooted in preconceived ideas.

In the psychological-progression pattern, therefore, the writer uses a technique called prolepsis; that is, he anticipates considerations that may pose barriers to acceptance of his central idea by dispensing with the reader's predisposition or logical and illogical objections before progressing to his conclusion or recommendation. The writer's intent is to create dissatisfaction with or at least uncertainty about existing perceptions of the subject as a prelude to providing what the writer believes is the best solution to the problem or answer to the question.

Suppose, for example, as a recently appointed manager, you inherited an operation in which a new system, requiring a high skill level, had been installed. After a short time on the job, you recognized that major problems had developed in the operation of the system because of inadequate training of operators. You therefore submit a request for additional funds to cover training of system operators. You know that the company is following a policy of stringent economy and that the person to whom you must justify the request has an obsession with maintaining operating costs at levels that are often unrealistic and suppressive.

You want to show that your request is in the company's best interest while addressing his obsession with cost reduction. Using the psychological-progressive pattern, you could introduce a variety of logical and illogical alternatives in a sequence such as the following:

1. Do not provide further training
2. Hire new people who are properly trained, to replace existing operators
3. Train everyone immediately
4. Train key people immediately

Your objective, of course, is to enhance the appeal of the alternative you believe to be best—in this instance, alternative 4. By placing it in perspective with other alternatives, you gradually narrow the choice.

THE FORMAT OF REPORTS

The patterns of organization we have been discussing are employed in the body of the report—that series of sections in which the detailed discussion of the central idea is developed. Because of the reader's "What's in it for me" motivation, however, every report should answer certain questions at the outset: why it was written, what considerations are involved, and, depending on the nature of the subject and the reader's attitude, what was found out or what is proposed.

In a long report, a summary is used to satisfy the reader's priorities of interest. The summary contains these elements:

Purpose

Scope

Findings or Conclusion(s)

Recommendation(s)

Not all reports contain both conclusion(s) and recommendation(s). Those that answer a question contain only findings or a conclusion; those that propose action contain recommendations.

In short reports, a discrete section labeled Summary is not employed. In fact, some short reports do not use headings to identify the elements of a summary. Nevertheless, the elements are included in the sequence listed above.

Statement of Purpose

Although the title of a large report or the subject line of a short report often suggests the purpose, most reports contain a more definitive statement of purpose. Depending on the reader's familiarity with the issue, the purpose may be stated after a brief history or background that places it in perspective:

> In-house fabrication of metals, optical filters, and moldings has become a rapidly expanding division of the company. Since this activity has been decentralized, it has become vital that we develop a system that measures the effectiveness of the processes we employ. This report analyzes a standard cost system.

When the reader does not need background, the purpose may be indicated in a simple reference to the request that prompted the report:

> As you requested, I looked into the various types of work performed in the Engineering Department to determine the kinds of space that will be required in the new building.

In either case, the purpose reveals immediately to the reader the significance of the subject and the implications of the information.

Statement of Scope

Although often overlooked, the scope is an important element of the report, for it determines the relevance of the information and the validity of the results. It defines the limits of the discussion, either by identifying the considerations included or by specifying those excluded. In a report in which the writer and reader agree in advance on the considerations to be included, the statement of scope is merely a reminder of the basis on which the results are founded. In reports in which the considerations are not mutually agreed on in advance, the statement of scope defines the boundaries so that any difference between what the reader expects to be covered and what is actually covered will not create misconception or raise questions.

In analytical reports, the scope may take the form of standards or criteria against which results are measured or assessed. In such instances, the scope may follow the statement of purpose:

Purpose

As the company has grown in size and complexity, the need for accurate and timely information has grown commensurately. To improve the efficiency of our reporting system, management is considering the installation of word-processing equipment incorporating the latest technology. This report evaluates the four leading models to determine their potential for satisfying our requirements.

Scope

The four models considered are Multipurpose 500, Magtex, Advanced Design, and Hopewell. Each was evaluated on its ease of operation, processing speed, reliability, capability of interfacing with our central computer, and cost.

In some reports, the scope is stated broadly and incorporated in the purpose.

This report summarizes the results of a study to determine the principal end uses of polystyrene during the next five years.

In short reports or memos, the scope of considerations may not be formally expressed, but is implied in the reasons given in support of the conclusion.

As you requested, I evaluated the facilities on Northside Highway as a potential location for our Research & Development activities.

These facilities do not meet our needs because:

1. They would require extensive and costly renovation;
2. They are inaccessible to public transportation; and
3. They would not allow space for orderly expansion.

Statements of Results or Action

These statements, frequently in the form of findings, conclusions, or recommendations, should normally appear after the purpose and scope have been defined. They state succinctly the pertinent facts and competent opinions that readers look for in helping them to understand the significance and implications of the issue or in making decisions. Because they are the most important statements in the report, they should be disclosed in the beginning of the report, where they will attract immediate attention.

Occasionally, of course, the writer may choose to delay introducing his results or suggested action. In a short report, for example, when he is certain the reader will read the entire report, the writer may choose to develop the discussion deductively and state his conclusion or recommendation as a logical outgrowth. Or, again, if he feels that the reader's preconceptions or other biases would prevent objective consideration of the results or suggested action, the writer may choose the psychological approach, which dispenses with these barriers before the writer's opinion or findings are introduced.

Other Preliminary Material

The writer may sometimes choose to include a separate section that lays the groundwork for what follows in the body of the report. The title of this section varies with the kind of material it contains. In a market study, for example, this section may define what segments have been included in the market; in a report dealing with a laboratory experiment, it may discuss the equipment and procedure used; in a report expected to get broad distribution, it may contain a detailed history of the problem or project; in a research report, it may discuss the method employed to gather information; and in a report to management, it may provide in layman's language a scientific, technological, or economic framework for the points developed later in the report.

In brief, the purpose, scope, and results take into consideration the reader's interests, whereas the other preliminary material takes into account his education, experience, and familiarity with the subject. The preliminary material attempts to bridge the gap between writer and reader so that the reader will better understand and appreciate the significance and implications of the facts and concepts contained in the detailed discussion.

The Body of the Report

The body is a generic term used to denote a number of specific sections with specific titles that encompass the detailed discussion of the report. The number of sections and the topics discussed are governed by the scope of considerations. For example, if you were asked to evaluate the desirability of a site as a location for a supermarket and had considered the population of the area, the traffic patterns, the accessibility of the site, competition, and cost of construction, the detailed discussion would encompass these five considerations. Consequently, the sections in the body of the report would be:

Population

Traffic Patterns

Accessibility

Competition

Cost

The sections in the body of the report provide the detailed evidence, documentation, and rationale. Objectivity and completeness, of course, require that both postitive and negative information be included. Therefore, whether or not each criterion or factor considered supports the general conclusion, its effect should be discussed.

Appendices

Material that may be helpful but not essential to an understanding of a subject—such as working memoranda, detailed statistics, supplementary tables, photographs, experimental details, and computations—may be relegated to an appendix. The information may be of interest only to certain specialists among the readers who wish to check a procedure or the derivation of a formula; or it may include products or applications screened but rejected. In a report to management, for example, three products with potential might be discussed in the body and twelve that failed to meet the criteria might be discussed briefly in the appendix.

Adaptability of Format

In essence, depending on the nature of the subject, the audience, and the writer's objective, the following format can be adapted to most short or long business and technical reports.

SUMMARY

    Purpose
    Scope
    Findings or Conclusion(s)
    Recommendation(s)

METHOD, HISTORY, Etc. (If needed)

BODY   { Separate Sections Treating Major Points in Detail

APPENDIX (If needed)

If you were writing a report involving one conclusion and all favorable statements, the Summary and overall organization might look something like this:

SUMMARY

Purpose and Scope

Because of the inevitable depletion of fossil fuel resources, industrialized nations have been searching for alternative energy sources. For years, the sun has been used successfully on an experimental scale to heat residential and commercial buildings. The purpose of this study was to determine whether solar climate control can be converted from an experimental success to a viable industry.

The study was limited to three considerations: technology, economics, and the potential market.

Conclusion

Solar climate control represents a potentially viable industry because:

1. The necessary technology is available;

2. The economics are becoming increasingly favorable; and

3. There is a large potential market.

Section Headings
  I. BACKGROUND (If needed)
  II. TECHNOLOGY
  III. ECONOMICS   }   BODY
  IV. POTENTIAL MARKET
    Appendix (If needed)

In a report involving analysis or evaluation, all the statements relating to the criteria or requirements on which the conclusion is based may not support the conclusion. Each criterion or requirement is weighted on the basis of its importance, and the algebraic sum of the weightings helps to determine whether the conclusion is positive or negative. Whether the statements support the conclusion or not, however, they must be included for the sake of objectivity and completeness.

The following summary and overall organization illustrate a situation in which one statement relating to the criteria (in this case, the one relating to the interest rates) is negative, but is offset by three that support the conclusion.

SUMMARY

Purpose and Scope

During the past fifteen months, Friendly Bank has been considering extending its market by placing greater emphasis on the southern portion of the state—specifically Region VIII. This report evaluates the feasibility of expanding branch lending activity in Region VIII.

The evaluation is based on a detailed analysis of the economic environment, present competition, market penetration, and interest rate considerations.

Conclusion

Although interest rates may not decrease by the anticipated 20 percent in 198__, expanding branch lending activity appears feasible because:

    1. The economic environment of the area is steadily improving and is suitable for commercial, residential, and industrial expansion;

    2. Competition within Region VIII is limited; and

3. Friendly Bank has 35 percent of the existing market, with a planned increase to 40 percent during next fiscal year.

Section Headings
  I. ECONOMIC ENVIRONMENT
  II. COMPETITION
  III. MARKET PENETRATION
  IV. INTEREST RATES

In still other instances, reports involve more than one conclusion because more than one question is asked. In the example below, the second conclusion is contingent on the first conclusion's being positive.

SUMMARY

Purpose and Scope

As the Glenview Manufacturing Company has grown, manual processing of its payroll has posed more and more problems. To overcome them, management asked us to determine the feasibility of automating the system and if automation proved feasible to determine the best operational alternative. This report details the results of our investigation.

To test whether automation is feasible, we evaluated the characteristics of the payroll system and the economics of automating it.

Conclusions
  1. Automating Glenview's payroll system is feasible because:
      a. The present system is already complex enough to justify such a move, and it will get even more complex; and
      b. The economics are favorable from the standpoints of initial cost and accrued savings.
  2. Off-site operation is preferable to in-house operation.

Section Headings
  I. CHARACTERISTICS OF SYSTEM
  II. ECONOMICS OF AUTOMATION
  III. OPERATIONAL ALTERNATIVES
      Appendix (If needed)

In a short report, the format might be adapted like this:

This report, submitted in response to your request last week, summarizes the results of a study to reduce the rising costs in the Installment Loan Department.

We can save at least $50,000 annually by:

1. Combining six jobs, and

2. Converting certain files to microfilm.

COMBINING JOBS

The pay-off function can be combined with the discount section. The evergreen collections can be combined with the control area collection department, and evergreen references can be combined with the main reference rotary files. If you approve changing the check guarantee from one year to three years, we shall merge the clerical function with the discount section. The billing section can be handled by the direct and indirect areas.

This combining of jobs will allow us to reduce our staff by nine people without hurting our efficiency.

The suggested reductions by area are:

Direct Area	3
Evergreen Section	2
Pay-Off Section	2
File Section	1
Billing Section	1

These reductions will save $45,000 per year.

MICROFILM

If we convert the open-credit reference file to microfilm, we will save 100 square feet of floor space at $25 per square foot. We will also realize savings by not having to search for files and by eliminating the need for file clerks.

Regardless of whether headings identify discussions of only a paragraph or two in short reports or of several pages in long reports, and regardless of whether a formal summary is identified in a long report or not identified in a short one, the sequence is essentially the same. So is the procedure for organizing them.

PROCEDURE

Before preparing a report, make sure you have gathered and analyzed all the information you need and have arrived at valid results. The reason many reports are poorly structured is that writers confuse the final presentation of the report with the written analysis of data they generate to reach the results they wish to report. Analysis precedes report preparation. The results of the analysis are the basis for the organization of a report.

When preparing lengthy reports, many writers expand on the details first and then write the summary. The summary therefore becomes a condensation of what is discussed in the body. Although a condensation or precis may satisfy the reader's needs to get an overview of what the report says, a mere shortening of the discussion is no guarantee that the reader's interests are served and that the report is organized effectively.

Therefore, in a report that is decision- or action-oriented, use this approach:

1. Write the purpose and the scope (if a scope is explicitly identified).

2. State the findings, conclusion(s), or recommendation(s).

3. Include after your conclusion(s) or recommendation(s) one statement (pro or con) relating to each item in the scope.

4. Provide as many sections in the body of the report as there are statements relating to items in the scope.

5. Outline each section of the body of the report.

EXERCISES

1. Which of the following are adequate themes?

   a. The advantages and disadvantages of no-fault insurance.

   b. Zero budgeting.

   c. The economic outlook is not promising.

   d. Salaries are ruining professional sports.

   e. Security problems in banks.

   f. Regulated prices.

g. Communication and good management are inseparable.

h. The energy crisis in the United States.

i. The feasibility of a four-day work week.

j. Meetings serve useful purposes.

2. What distinguishes themes from nonthemes? What is the value of a theme? Where should it appear in a report?

3. Revise the following summary and report outline to reflect a more concise and cohesive view of the operation.

SUMMARY

Purpose and Scope

Management asked for a review of the Metropole operation for the 1978 - 79 season. All pertinent aspects of the operation were to be included.

Approach

In carrying out this assignment, we:

1. Discussed variances versus plan with location and regional management.

2. Analyzed control and reporting procedures.

3. Analyzed the lease agreement to isolate factors that may affect financial performance.

4. Determined the high cost of food.

5. Investigated possible savings in operating expenses.

6. Reviewed actual versus projected staffing levels.

7. Plan to make specific recommendations and discuss them with regional management to obtain their agreement.

Conclusions

The product cost was 10 percent higher than projected. The variance was primarily caused by poor security and inadequate food and beverage controls.

No provision was made in the plan for the cost of cleaning all food service areas as required by the lease agreement. Total cost for 1978-79 was $18,800 or 2.1 percent of sales.

Sales reporting was handled inaccurately, resulting in product cost distortions in several categories.

Sales tax was not backed out from sales of alcoholic beverages.

Metropole's remote location has resulted in serious labor shortages. If additional employee housing is not constructed, the labor situation will continue to have a negative impact on the operation.

In the 1978–79 season, Metropole experienced an operating loss of $11,900, or 1.2 percent, compared with a planned profit of $93,200, or 11.3 percent.

    I. OVERVIEW
      A. Performance vs Plan
      B. Projections
    II. FINANCIAL EVALUATION
      A. Product Cost
      B. Payroll
      C. Operating Expenses
    III. LEASE ANALYSIS
      A. Definition of Lease Terms
      B. Factors Affecting Performance

---

4. Write an evaluation of the following summary. Stress the clarity of the purpose and scope, the relevance of the conclusions, the information that is missing.

SUMMARY

Purpose and Scope

As a result of development work by the Bigelow Corporation, a water electrolysis cell could be manufactured that would provide hydrogen with total impurities not exceeding one part per million from a unit of smaller size than any other electrolysis cell.

Empirical Research Associates was asked to determine the size of the present market for high-purity hydrogen in four industrial sectors in the United States, to forecast future demand, and to estimate the possible market share which could be obtained by the Bigelow high-purity hydrogen generator. The benefits of "on-site" generation of gas, consistency of supply and quality, and possible price advantages were to be taken into account. ERA's judgments of the reactions of existing hydrogen suppliers or companies that could market similar systems were to be incorporated.

The four industries to be investigated were semiconductor, pharmaceutical, food processing, and specialty gases.

Conclusions

1. The requirements for very high-purity hydrogen in the United States can be met by using evaporated liquid hydrogen. When liquid hydrogen cannot be used because of distance from a source of supply or local laws forbidding its use in urban areas, methods of obtaining the necessary purity levels are available (mainly palladium diffusers and cryogenic cold traps).

2. The requirements of the Air Force and the N.A.S.A. led to the development of the necessary techniques to manufacture and handle liquid hydrogen on a substantial scale (some 160 tons per day). These requirements have been reduced. Consequently, there is ready availability of the liquid, price competition is apparent, and the pattern of declining prices is similar to the historic situation for each of oxygen, nitrogen, and argon.

3. The supply of hydrogen gas by a common pipeline to a number of different users has started in east Texas. The manufacturing process is from natural gas, the product is of high purity and is approaching the price of 3.5 cents per 100 standard cubic feet (S.C.F.) at usage rates of 10,000,000 S.C.F. per day.

4. The manufacture of chlorine and caustic soda gives a by-product hydrogen that can be readily and cheaply purified. As it is in the gaseous form, the use tends to be localized because of the high cost of transportation due to the weight of the pressure container.

5. The largest use of hydrogen is for the manufacture of ammonia, followed in size by refining operations (hydrofining and hydrotreating), then by the manufacture of methanol and other petrochemical operations. The usage of hydrogen of better than 99.5 percent purity for other purposes is estimated at 30 billion standard cubic feet per year. Approximately 20 percent is manufactured for captive use, 43 percent is sold and delivered by pipeline to separate consumers, and the remainder delivered in cylinders, large tube trailers, and as liquid.

6. The growth in demand for 99.5 percent or better purity hydrogen has averaged 17.5 percent per year for the last four years and will probably grow at an annual rate of 15 percent per year at least until 1980. However, the largest proportion

of the growth will be taken by hydrogen manufactured from hydrocarbons.

7. The electronics industry in the United States used an estimated 400 million S.C.F. of high-purity hydrogen in 1968. This requirement will increase by some 20 percent per year at least until 1980. The price range for delivered hydrogen was 35 cents to $1.60 per 100 S.C.F., and the weighted average was 42.5 cents.

8. The pharmaceutical industry in the United States probably used not more than 15 million S.C.F. of hydrogen in 1967, for manufacturing pharmaceutical materials.

All present usages are for batch reactions that are not performed on a regular basis. Much of the use is for hydrogenation reactions that require gas at up to 1,200 p.s.i.g.

Because of these operational factors, we do not consider that the Bigelow generator would be of use or economically justifiable to a manufacturer of pharmaceuticals.

---

5. Reorganize the following memo and make it concise.

In order to improve the Security Vault operation, one of the major problems facing us concerns personnel. It is my intention to recommend transfers in this area to take effect as rapidly as possible.

However, we cannot continue to deplete our present staff without replacements, and we can only submit one name at a time for transfer as a replacement has been received.

In January, 198__, one man retired and in March another employee left the Bank. In addition, two men have been assigned to do customer verifications — a newly created job here.

On February 18, 198__, I submitted a requisition for a man to replace Arthur Jones (retired 1/31/8__) and on March 10, 198__, submitted another requisition for a man to replace John Doe (left Bank 3/11/8__). When these two men are replaced, we can then proceed to make additional changes.

In addition, I propose to requisition two men to implement the present Collateral Vault staff to improve dual-control, which management wants and which Auditor is in the process of commenting on in a lengthy report to Mr. B.

For handling securities running into the billions of dollars, I am strongly opposed to hiring agency personnel (such as Agency X), summer replacements (such as students), and part-time employees, except for a few selected retirees who seek employment after retirement.

The caliber of people employed must be carefully chosen, and their backgrounds carefully checked out—probably by our Security Officer. Personnel with health problems (I believe we now have about eleven in this category) should not be hired and personnel "who haven't made it" in other departments should not be sent to us.

The IQ of new employees should be sufficiently high so that they recognize the responsibility of handling securities, many of which are payable to bearer. Possibly the Job Evaluation people should review the job ranges of all vault positions.

Because of the possibility of creating a bad morale factor that could result from a "leak" to the vault personnel of impending changes, I would prefer to discuss suggested changes with you, one of your staff, and/or with the Personnel Department.

I have some definite opinions regarding some of the vault personnel, formed from talking to the Supervisors and from my personal observation—again to be discussed confidentially.

3
Outlining: Building the Framework

Ask any report writer whether he outlines before he writes, and he will probably say that he does. Yet many writers who are convinced that they prepare an outline in reality do not. They create only the illusion of one.

Some, for example, simply jot down broad topics of discussion, such as the following:

Introduction

Market Definition

Analytical Approach

Interpretation of Data

Results

Such an "outline," however, is at best a table of contents. It may be convenient for readers who wish to locate a type of information, but it is of little or no help to those who wish to prepare information. It is too broad to be of any value. It is the product of ritual rather than of need.

An outline is essentially the visual extension of thinking. Its function is to help in recording, grouping, screening, weighting, and sequencing ideas in accordance with the organizational pattern that the writer decides is most appropriate. The need for an outline varies with the complexity of the report and the writer's capacity to envision and remember detail completely and logically. The outline may be as simple as a few notes or as detailed as a series of topics and subtopics with important ideas highlighted in topic sentences.

THE INFORMAL OUTLINE

For letters, memoranda, and short reports, an informal outline may be all that is necessary. The informal outline consists of notes than can be easily expanded. These notes are used primarily to ensure that the writer responds to the questions or issues. For example, in responding to the letter below, your outline might consist only of the pencilled notes jotted down on the bottom of the letter:

Dear Mr. Parker:

I recently spoke with Jim Dudly, who suggested that you might be interested in addressing the Belvidere Chapter of the National Association of Accountants.

We would be pleased if you would address the meeting of our chapter on Wednesday, April 20, 19____. We'll accept any topic you choose.

The meeting will be held at the Belvidere Motor Inn, Belvidere, CT. A fellowship hour will begin at 6:00 P.M., followed by dinner and the introduction of our guest speaker.

If you accept our invitation, please send me a brief writeup of your background, which will be included in our program booklet.

We look forward to hearing from you.

1. will accept
2. topic will be...
3. time free, expenses not
4. send directions

Sincerely

P.D. Allison
Program Director

The informal outline is simple and convenient, but it has limitations. In essence, it is a vehicle merely for recording ideas and arranging them fairly quickly in a sequence appropriate to the writer's objective. Because of its limitations, however, it should be used only when the objective and the issue(s) are straightforward and uncomplicated.

THE FORMAL OUTLINE

When you are structuring a lengthy or complex report, the sheer number of ideas can create a problem as you attempt to classify them, determine their relevance, and establish their relationship and relative importance. Consequently, you need a vehicle that will allow you not only to record and screen ideas, but also to weigh, group, and arrange them in an appropriate sequence. The formal outline is useful in such circumstances.

A formal outline can consist of words, phrases, or sentences, or of a combination of the three. Whether you restrict the outline to words and phrases or whether you combine words and phrases with topic sentences depends on the level of detail and constraints you need to ensure completeness, coherence, and emphasis in the structural arrangement.

The Topical Outline

Consisting of words and phrases, the topical outline is useful in establishing appropriate emphasis and logical progression by showing the grouping of topics, their rank, and their arrangement. In the sample topical outlines shown below, note that although the same topics are included in both outlines, the emphasis in Outline A is different from that in Outline B because the groupings and rankings are different.

Outline A	Outline B
I. Operational Alternatives	I. Operational Alternatives
A. In-House Operation	A. Equipment
1. Equipment	1. In-House
2. Personnel Requirements	2. Off-Site
3. Costs	B. Personnel Requirements
B. Off-Site Operation	1. In-House
1. Equipment	2. Off-Site
2. Personnel Requirements	C. Costs
3. Costs	1. In-House
	2. Off-Site

Which of the two outlines is more appropriate depends on the objective of the writer. Outline A emphasizes types of operation, whereas Outline B emphasizes components of the operations.

To make certain that the selection and arrangement of detail are in keeping with your objective, it is necessary to keep in mind the idea you want to point up. Although the central idea is the focus of every report, in long or complex reports it may be supported by subordinate ideas, which, in turn, govern the structure of the discussions contained in the various sections. For example, in Chapter 2, we showed a sample summary of a report on solar climate control. The conclusion was:

> Solar climate control represents a potentially viable industry because:
>
> 1. The necessary technology is available;
>
> 2. The economics are becoming increasingly more favorable; and
>
> 3. There is a large potential market.

Each of the three supporting statements represents a subordinate idea or theme that becomes the basis for an outline. Here, for example, is how topical outlines based on the three statements above might appear. The subordinate ideas are in parentheses to remind you of what the outline is designed to point up.

I. TECHNOLOGY
(The necessary technology is available)
A. Solar Collectors
   1. Design Criteria
   2. Types
B. Solar Air Condition-
   ing
C. Thermal Storage
D. On-Site Power
   1. Solar Cells
   2. Solar-Powered
      Heat Engines

II. ECONOMICS
(The economics are becoming increasingly more favorable)
A. Energy Demand
   1. Electricity
   2. Natural Gas
   3. Oil
B. Fuel Availability
C. Fuel Prices
D. Government Action
E. Outlook for Solar
   Energy

III. POTENTIAL MARKET
(There is a large poten-
tial market)
A. Residential Buildings
   1. Single-Family
   2. Multiple Dwellings
B. Commercial Build-
   ings
C. Government Build-
   ings

Even though the topical outline helps you to categorize and arrange detail in accordance with a theme, it is still fairly general. Consequently, when you begin to write the report, you will need to decide on the specific details you want to include and where you want to introduce them. In effect, the topical outline still leaves gaps in the structure of a report.

If the report is not too long or complex, you may be able to supply the specific details as you write. If you are dealing with copious detail or complex relationships, however, you will find the detailed outline most useful.

Detailed Outline

The detailed outline combines words, phrases, and topic sentences. It is useful not only for grouping, ranking, and arranging topics but also for showing the level of detail to be used in the elaboration of each topic.

The example shown below is a detailed outline of the Section I outline shown on the facing page.

I. TECHNOLOGY

    A. Solar Collectors

        Solar Collectors, by virtue of their geometry or surface properties, absorb and trap solar energy and impart it to a heat-transfer fluid that circulates through the collector.

        1. Design Criteria

        The cover panes should have high transmittance to solar energy and low transmittance to reradiated infrared energy.

        The absorber should resist corrosion, be compatible with the heat-transfer fluid, and permit application of the desired surface coating.

        The heat-transfer fluid should function properly and without degradation at all temperatures, be noncorrosive, and pose no safety hazard.

        2. Types

        The flat-plate collector is the most common type.

        Other collectors having characteristics similar to those of the flat-plate type are also available commercially.

Advanced concepts are in the prototype development stage.

B. Solar Air Conditioning

Absorption machines represent the best developed heat-actuated air-conditioning technology.

Heat engines based on the Rankine cycle are good candidates for solar climate control air conditioning.

Systems that use solid or liquid desiccants that can be regenerated by solar heat are also being considered.

C. Thermal Storage

Thermal storage materials fall into two main categories: (1) specific heat materials and (2) change-of-phase material.

For the near term, at least, specific heat storage materials are preferable.

Change-of-phase materials are of particular interest when heat is to be stored at a very narrow temperature interval with high volumetric heat capacity.

They have posed a great many unresolved problems.

D. On-Site Power

1. Solar Cells

Single-crystal silicon offers several advantages for use in solar cells.

Other materials, especially cadmium sulfide, are being considered.

2. Solar-Powered Heat Engines

Most attention in this area has been focused on the Rankine-cycle heat engines using both water and organic working fluids.

The size of the collector array and therefore the cost of the power produced will be greatly influenced by the thermal efficiency of the system.

To achieve efficiencies comparable to those achieved with silicon, solar cells will require advanced solar collectors such as those using a partial vacuum to eliminate convection losses.

The detailed outline offers several advantages. First, it helps you to avoid including digression and unimportant information because it gives you a chance to screen ideas and view them in relation to the topic being discussed. Second, it provides a rough gauge of the number of paragraphs you plan to devote to the development of each topic because each sentence included in the detailed outline represents the topic sentence of a paragraph: thus, you can decide whether the planned development is commensurate with the importance you have assigned to each topic. Third, it establishes much more discipline and hence precise relationships than words or phrases alone; therefore, it provides extra insurance against lack of coherence. Fourth, it shows the logic of the progression of thought units. Fifth, it allows you to concentrate on developing ideas instead of attempting to select, arrange, and develop ideas simultaneously in the expansion of an outline into a complete report. Finally, it allows you to begin preparing the draft at whatever point is easiest and most convenient for you.

PROCEDURE

It is foolish to believe that you can prepare an outline without revision. An outline grows piecemeal. Ideas do not always occur in any logical sequence. Consequently, in recording ideas and ensuring that the relevant ones are arranged in an appropriate sequence, you might find that because of numerous revisions, an outline developed on an 8½-by-11-inch sheet of paper looks like a can of worms. Phrases and sentences are scratched out, sweeping arrows indicate the new location of an idea, afterthoughts are jotted down along the margins, new versions of ideas are written between lined-out older versions, and the product itself is difficult to read and follow.

One way of overcoming this problem is to use either 3-by-5-inch cards or to cut up sheets of 8½-by-11-inch paper into five strips and to record one idea to a card or a strip. In this way, you can treat the ideas as a deck of cards and sort them. Deleting an idea becomes simply a matter of placing the card to one side; adding an idea merely requires filling out another card or strip; and ideas can be rearranged easily by simply shifting and reshifting the cards. When the arrangement suits you and you feel the outline is complete, you can copy it onto a full-sized sheet of paper for easier reference.

In preparing a detailed outline, you may also find the following procedure helpful:

1. Write down the subordinate theme to be developed.
2. Using the key words in the theme, select topics that amplify on them.
3. In view of the reader's needs and attitude as well as your objective, decide which should be the principal topics and which the subordinate topics, and arrange them in order of importance.
4. Write down amplifying topic sentences as they occur to you.
5. Screen out and shift sentences until you are satisfied that they progress logically, cohesively, and convincingly.
6. Note where you plan to insert tabular and graphical material as part of the development of ideas.

By following this procedure for each section of the report, you will have prepared an outline in which each successive coordination and subordination insures that the section themes are enhanced. Since the themes of each section in turn point up the main theme, the entire report will be focused properly.

THE OUTLINE AS A TOOL FOR REVIEW

Many reports require approval before they are distributed. Before receiving approval, they are reviewed for content, structure, and other considerations by one person or more, usually when the report has been worked over extensively and is considered to be in final form. At that stage, however, a review for content and structure often creates as many problems as it solves. In many instances, the procedure is inefficient; and in most, it is frustrating to the writer. It is inefficient because: (1) a great many changes involving deletion, addition, and rearrangement of material are often recommended after the writer has spent considerable time and effort in developing and polishing the exposition; and (2) those people whose function is to evaluate content or structure frequently become diverted and, with little to recommend them as stylists, tamper with the structure of sentences. It is frustrating because when the review is delayed until this stage, there is usually little time left to incorporate the suggested revisions and still meet the deadline; consequently, the final product does not always reflect the writer's best effort.

It is often more effective, therefore, to review long or complex reports in stages. In the first stage, the review should focus on content, the logic of the structure, and the planned depth of detail. For this review, the detailed outline is most helpful because:

1. Isolating the elements of principal importance in the review makes them easier to review;

2. Providing only heading and topic sentences prevents reviewers from wasting time tampering with the structure of sentences;

3. Eliminating the need for a finished draft at this stage helps the writer to be more amenable to suggested revisions, since he does not feel "locked" into the exposition; and

4. It allows time to reconcile conflicting recommended revisions when more than one reviewer is involved.

After the outline is approved, the writer can approach the preparation of the draft with confidence. Although in the editorial review at a later stage the draft may be revised slightly, the need for major revision has been reduced to zero.

EXERCISES

1. Evaluate the following proposed outline.

GROWTH AND EXPANSION OF NHL

During the last year, a study has been done to determine if the NHL has overexpanded in its quest for recognition.

It has been determined that with the expansion of the NHL and also the introduction of the WHA there has been a depletion of hockey talent to supply all the teams. Also it has created more of a bargaining potential for the players, creating high-salaried players.

1. The original NHL consisted of three Canadian teams.

2. The first expansion of the NHL took place in the 40's, which saw the NHL expand to an 8-team, 2-division league.

3. The second expansion took place in the 60's, which saw 6 more teams added and divided into two divisions.

4. The third expansion took place in the early 70's, which saw two more American teams added.

5. The fourth expansion of the NHL took place also in the 70's and saw two more American teams added and the league broken up into 4 divisions.

6. The introduction of the WHA, which also took place in the 70's, created more lack of talented players and made bargaining for players unrealistic.

---

2. Arrange the following list into a series of headings and subheadings to form a topical outline of the major sections of a report dealing with glass containers.

Drinking Glasses	Convenience
Equipment	Cost
Pet Shops	Design Criteria
Usefulness	Radio Commercials
Newspaper Advertisements	Sales Outlets
Discount Houses	Department Stores
Economy	Production Considerations
Aquarium Tanks	Circulars
Labor	Bottles
Novelty Shops	Promotion
Common Types	

3. You have been involved in a study to determine the best location for a new regional community college. You collected the following information. Prepare an expanded outline of the information.

   1. The state's population in 1960, 2.5 million people, is expected to reach nearly 3.5 million by 1980, and roughly 5 million by the year 2000.

   2. Where the population lives is the most significant single factor in determining the location of a community college.

   3. About one-fourth of all community college students are between the ages of 26 and 40.

   4. The changing composition of the labor force reflects the transition from a manufacturing to a service economy.

   5. Nearly all full-time students are single; about one-third of the part-time students are married.

   6. By the year 2000, more than 98 percent of the population will reside in urban areas, and there will be only 50 or so towns with a population of fewer than 10,000 persons.

   7. Community colleges should be established in urban areas having substantial economic activity.

   8. This state ranks first in the nation in per capita income: in 1960 it was $2,863, compared to $2,200 for the nation as a whole. The state's median family income in 1960 was $7,000.

   9. The characteristics of community college students vary more

widely than those of any other student body in the higher education system.

10. In 1960, employment in the state was approximately 1 million; by 1980, it is expected to grow to roughly 1.5 million; and it will reach more than 2 million by the year 2000.

11. Since a large portion of the students enrolled at a community college will work (about 57 percent), it is important to locate the school in an area in which jobs are plentiful.

12. Even in urban areas, most students drive to community colleges rather than use public transportation.

13. In 1960, 40 percent of the state's labor force was engaged in manufacturing; 58 percent was employed in the service sector.

14. Two-year colleges serve two distinct populations: (1) the college-age youths of 17 to 21 and (2) students age 26 to 40 who have returned to school to learn new skills or upgrade present skills.

15. Fifty-seven percent of all community college students hold part-time jobs consuming between 17 and 22 hours per week.

16. More part-time than full-time students come from families in which the head of the household has a high school education or less.

17. The location of existing institutions of higher education, such as state colleges and universities, will affect any decision on where new community colleges will be located.

18. About one-half of the students in community colleges attend school part-time.

4. Select a subject related to your job. Prepare a summary, and prepare a detailed outline of the body of the report.

4
Preparing the Draft: Points About Procedure

If you are like most writers, you are convinced that the difficult part of writing is getting started—a fact you probably attribute to your lack of writing skill. But difficulty in getting started frequently has little or nothing to do with lack of skill; it is usually the result of lack of preparation. When ideas do not come easily or at all, perhaps it is because you have not collected enough information; when you have a problem sorting out ideas, perhaps it is because you have not spent enough time analyzing your information; and when you have trouble deciding where or whether information should be included, you may not have spent enough time organizing your ideas. In essence, the difficulty stems from trying to do too many things at one time.

While recognizing that you can overcome a great deal of difficulty by adopting a one-step-at-a-time approach, you should also keep in mind that the purpose of the first draft is to expand your outline. It is merely a vehicle for capturing ideas that relate to the topic sentences contained in your outline. Recognizing the purpose of the first draft, therefore, you may find the following suggestions helpful.

Pick a Quiet Place to Prepare the Draft
John Ruskin, the nineteenth-century English writer, art critic, and social reformer, published circulars to discourage interruptions when he sat down to do some serious writing. They read: "Mr. J. Ruskin is about to begin a work of great importance and therefore begs that in reference to calls and correspondence you will consider him dead for the next two months."

Although you may not be able or even need to closet yourself from your normal activities for two months so that you can prepare a report, you do need an environment that is not distractive. It is difficult to prepare a fairly long or complex report amidst continual interruptions: telephone calls, visitors, meetings, queries. A draft report cannot be developed during coffee breaks, between meetings, or over the conversation rising above the partitions of modular office arrangements. It requires quiet and concentration.

If your normal work environment is a handicap, reserve a conference room or stay home while you prepare the draft. Trying to write reports after hours is not always a solution because the pressures and rigor of your daily activity may be mentally fatiguing, and fatigue hampers creativity. Therefore, devoting the morning hours to preparing a report may be more productive than delaying it until evening. And a few hours out of the office may accomplish as much as a few days in it.

Prepare Sections in Increasing Order of Difficulty

Most writers prepare the parts of a report in the sequence in which they ultimately appear. Consequently, any difficulty they encounter with an early section delays the whole report, and the resulting time constraint may even interfere with their ability to do an effective job on subsequent sections that pose no problem.

The fixed-sequence approach is self-defeating if you have prepared a detailed outline. A writer who has a detailed outline is like a home builder with the foundation in place: he can begin construction any place he chooses. Selecting the easiest first and finishing it quickly may create a sense of accomplishment. And although working on the most difficult part last will not eliminate the difficulty, recognizing that you have only one part to complete may give you a psychological lift and substantially reduce the difficulty.

Use Topic Sentences as Hangers for Associated Ideas

As one thought generates another in the development of topic sentences into paragraphs, make sure that each thought relates to and advances the idea expressed in the topic sentence it is intended to expand. If you do not remind yourself every once in a while what point you are trying to develop, you may go off on a tangent and defeat your purpose. If you are not certain whether a thought relates to the topic idea, include it and decide on its relevance later. Pausing at this stage to make fine decisions about relevance may interrupt the flow of ideas so important to expansion. Furthermore, it is easier to delete than to add when revising the draft later.

Get Your Ideas Down Quickly

Whether you choose to dictate or write your rough draft, prepare it quickly to take advantage of the associations prompted by each new thought. Therefore, you might want to consider dictating the draft instead of writing it. According to the Department of Labor, using a dictating machine allows you to record ideas up to six times faster than writing, and dictating to a stenographer is up to three times faster than writing.

One important advantage of dictating is that we are much more fluent when we talk than when we write. When we talk, we are concerned more with thoughts than with words. When we write, however, words become important. We try to impress by using big words—as though the reader measures the profundity of the thought by the size of the words. Did you ever notice, for example, that *sufficient* is almost invariably used instead of *enough* in writing? In fact, some writers, in an attempt to be even more impressive, merely become redundant by replacing *enough* with *sufficiently adequate.*

Since your principal concern in preparing a rough draft is to capture ideas, don't worry about diction, grammar, punctuation, or sentence structure. Ideas are often elusive; consequently, it is far better to record them even in rough form than to allow them to escape while you search for the precise word or construction. Of course, it is important to express your ideas as clearly as you can without slowing the pace of your thoughts. It is of dubious value to jot down an idea in language that will have little meaning later. At this stage, simple direct sentences (subject-verb-object pattern) are preferable to complex constructions because when revising, you will find it easier to establish proper relationships between ideas simply expressed than to segregate ideas confusingly or improperly related.

Do Not Try to Write and Edit at the Same Time

Writing is a creative effort; editing, a critical one. You cannot do both simultaneously because they require different faculties and different temperaments. If you try to polish your sentences as you go along, you interrupt the association of ideas, which is the basis of creativity. While you are trying to revise an earlier sentence, you allow a new thought to escape. When you finish editing the earlier sentence, you then waste considerable time trying to recall the thought that was on the tip of your mind before you began the disruptive editing. Sometimes you never recall the thought. Even worse, if you do recall it, you are always convinced that in its second coming it isn't conceived half as brilliantly as it was in the original version that you allowed to escape.

Here, again, dictation has an advantage over writing. Because you cannot see what you dictate, you will be less likely to be distracted by what you have recorded.

Let Your Thoughts Flow Until You Run Out of Ideas

If you are preparing a letter or memorandum, dictate or write from beginning to end without interruption. If you are preparing a long report, compose the draft until you deplete the wellspring of ideas. When you become mentally fatigued or when you lose the creative momentum, stop at a convenient place such as at the end of a section or subsection. That is why using statements supporting your main conclusion as subordinate themes governing sections of the report and treating sections as miniature reports helps you to divide your textual development into workable, energy-conserving units.

5
Orderly Development: The Paragraph Principle

To write reports effectively, you must tailor information to the reader. Tailoring is largely a matter of quantity and pace. It involves providing the amount and level of detail commensurate with the reader's needs and regulating the flow of information according to the difficulty of the subject matter and the reader's capacity to process and store information. Paragraphs, therefore, are important tailoring tools because, properly designed, they convey information in easily assimilated units.

Although we usually think in sentences, we explain in paragraphs. If, however, we prepared our explanations as pages of uninterrupted text, the sheer number of ideas that the reader would have to deal with would pose a problem. If the discussion were complex and weighty, the problem would be compounded. To help the reader grasp them easily, principal ideas must be identified and enhanced by related detail. To help the reader consider the implication and importance of the dominant ideas and place them in perspective, paragraphs must be long enough to provide clear and complete development but short enough to allow for convenient pauses for recapitulation and reflection. To ensure easy assimilation, therefore, paragraphs should have unity, completeness, coherence, and impact.

UNITY

Unity means simply that every paragraph should be built on one principal idea embodied in the topic sentence. This idea establishes the relevance of every other idea in the paragraph. No detail, regardless of its interest or educational value, should be included unless it relates to and advances the main idea. Every sentence in a paragraph, therefore, radiates from the main idea, or topic sentence, and amplifies on it until the paragraph is logically and factually complete.

Unity thus contributes to ease of comprehension. Note, for example, how each supporting sentence contributes to the main idea (stated in the first sentence) in the paragraph below.

> Applying saliva or toothpaste to the inner surface of the glass plate of scuba divers' masks is not a satisfactory solution to the problem of severe fogging. These substances do not prevent moisture. Rather, they merely cause the moisture to form a continuous and transparent film that does not last long. It is replaced by fogging, especially in cold water and if the diver breathes a great deal of moist air from the atmosphere instead of the dry air from his tanks. Consequently, to overcome the fogging, the diver must surface frequently, flush his mask, and apply more toothpaste or saliva.

By contrast, note in the following paragraph how despite the simplicity of each idea, the lack of unity interferes with the reader's ability to put his finger quickly on the main point the author is trying to make. You may think the paragraph is easy to read and that you know what it says. But try to express the main idea in one sentence. You'll find that you can't unless you incorporate practically every idea in the paragraph. Although the sentences appear to form a paragraph, at least four of them are competing for dominance. And instead of supporting one main idea, each thought is stated as a kind of self-evident truth that requires no further explanation.

> Writing is one of the most important skills in any business. Clear writing is no accident. Few people have the natural ability to write well. It can be learned. The rewards for communication through the printed word are great for those who make the effort.

Because disparate thoughts are irrelevant or extraneous when compressed into a single paragraph does not mean that they should be eliminated from further consideration in the report. They may very well deserve to be included as topic sentences of other paragraphs. For example, the sentences in the nonunified paragraph above could be arranged as topic ideas in a continuing discussion of Writing Skills. As main ideas in a series of paragraphs, they could appear in the following sequence:

- Writing is one of the most important skills in any business.
- Good writing is not accidental.
- Although difficult for many, it is a skill that can be learned.

• For those who make the effort, the rewards are great.

Viewing the ideas from this perspective, the writer can more easily recognize that each one would be more readily understood and accepted if supported by further detail. In essence, what was once a paragraph is now a topic-sentence outline that lays the foundation for four paragraphs.

Without a clear-cut topic idea, writers frequently pile sentence on sentence, hoping that a dominant idea will emerge. The problem with this approach, of course, is that it is more useful in preparing an outline than in developing a paragraph. If a topic idea does emerge and the writer still wants to prepare a unified paragraph instead of an outline, he must eliminate some of the thoughts, regroup others, and perhaps even add detail.

Most writers do not take the trouble to revise paragraphs even if the point they wanted to make does emerge eventually. In fact, most writers of the free-association-of-ideas school do not worry about whether a dominant idea appears. They believe they have a general idea of what they want to say, and whether they say it precisely does not bother them. As a result, they write all around the subject without ever getting to the heart of the matter. The result of this approach is shown below on the left—two undeveloped and confusing "paragraphs."

It is far better to invest extra time at the outset to crystallize the major idea you want to point up in each paragraph and use it to provide focus and direction. Note that the paragraph on the right below begins with a topic sentence that has been carefully considered. With that idea delineated, the details scattered through the two paragraphs on the left can be rearranged into one factually and logically complete paragraph.

Original	Revised
The selling price for a new dwelling unit is based on many factors, supply-demand relationships, various profits, financing costs, and the cost of the structure (the construction contract value) to the developer. Technology can only affect the last of these factors; the others are largely responsible for the current high costs of housing. The construction cost represents 50 to 75 percent of the sale price,	The best way to reduce the monthly carrying costs for housing is not by advancements in technology, but by reductions in the cost of money and the cost of land. For example, if a dwelling unit sold for $20,000, the buyer would pay $142 per month for a 25-year, 7 percent mortgage with no down payment. For a unit such as this, the construction cost would be about $12,000. If better technology could reduce this cost

depending on other variables; a 10 percent cost saving in construction would reflect a 5 to 7.5 percent saving in the purchase price.

For example, if a dwelling unit selling for $20,000 costs $12,000 to build (excluding land, services, profits, sales costs), an owner would pay $142 per month for a 25-year, 7 percent mortgage with no down payment. If technology could reduce the building cost by $1200, or 10 percent, the monthly payment would be reduced by 5 percent, to $134. However, if the interest rate were lowered to 3 percent and the mortgage extended to 30 years, monthly carrying costs would be reduced 40 percent, to $84, and 1 percent money would reduce monthly costs to $64. If rapidly inflating land costs could be subsidized and/or leased, additional order of magnitude savings in monthly costs could be achieved.

as much as 10 percent ($1200), the carrying cost would drop only 5 percent, to $134. If, however, the interest rate were lowered to 3 percent and the mortgage were extended to 30 years, the monthly carrying costs would be reduced 40 percent, to $84. An interest rate of 1 percent would reduce monthly costs to $64. Furthermore, similar savings would be possible if the rapidly inflating land costs could be offset through a subsidy or a lease arrangement.

When the topic thought is established, the sentences that expand on it are simply subordinated to it in the development of a paragraph. In essence, then, a paragraph is nothing more than a detailed outline carried to its ultimate level of specificity and subordination. For example, in the detailed outline shown in Chapter 3 (p. 36) the two topic sentences shown in D-1 could have been expanded further, as follows:

D. On-Site Power
    1. Solar Cells

   • Single-crystal silicon offers several advantages for use in solar cells.

        It has a high efficiency: 14 percent is reached routinely and as high as 20 percent occasionally.

It has good resistance to severe environmental conditions such as thermal cycling.

It has high reliability and stable long-term performance.

Its cost may be reduced substantially if it is mass-produced.

- Other materials, especially cadmium sulfide, are being considered.

Among the other materials being considered are gallium-arsenide and organics.

Thin-film cadmium sulfide cells, however, have received the most attention because of their potentially low lost.

The performance of these cells, particularly their long-term reliability, moisture and temperature sensitivity, and potential efficiency, however, needs to be improved.

The vertical arrangement of the outline is simply replaced with a horizontal arrangement to provide conventional paragraph form in the final report. Paragraphing viewed from this perspective may be helpful to some writers, because when sentences are arranged vertically instead of horizontally, those that do not belong or that are in the wrong sequence can sometimes be detected more easily. If you find this approach helpful, try preparing paragraphs vertically. When you are satisfied with the selection and arrangement of detail, it is a simple matter to convert the sentences into a horizontal alignment.

The topic thought can be either expressed or implied. It is usually expressed when the main idea is an opinion, concept, assumption, conclusion, or some other statement that requires qualification, justification, or explanation. We have seen several examples of expressed topic sentences in earlier examples; here is another. (The topic thought is underscored for your convenience.)

A tape recorder can be very helpful in business. For the engineer invited to a plant to observe new procedures, processes, or equipment, a tape recorder can help gather the information that his host supplies; in so doing it eliminates the need for note-taking, which can be distracting. For the interviewer, the tape recorder can be used to record what the prospective employee had to say about interests and abilities. For the person asked to take minutes at a meeting, the tape recorder is a means of ensuring an accurate report of the details because it allows you to record everything and edit out what is unimportant. Finally, the person who travels a great deal can record notes or dictate memos and reports on the plane or in the hotel room while the details are still fresh in his or her mind and thus save time later at the office.

Topic sentences are often implied when a description or a definition is involved. In the following description, the implied topic sentence is *Here is how hemodialysis, or an artificial kidney, works.*

> When a person's kidney fails to function, an artificial kidney is used to keep the patient alive. Usually blood from the patient's arm is pumped into a disposable artificial kidney, where it flows over the surface of the membrane. On the other side of the membrane is a balanced electrolyte solution, the dialysate. Water, urea, and other materials diffuse across the membrane from the blood into this solution. The cleansed blood returns to the patient, and the dialysate is ultimately discarded. The procedure takes four to eight hours and must be repeated two or three times a week in some cases.

Whether expressed or implied in the final document, the topic idea should always be expressed in your outline. When you are developing the paragraph, it serves as a reminder of the point you wish to elaborate on. When you are reviewing and editing the draft later, it serves as a reference to determine whether you focused on the idea you wanted to.

From the standpoint of rhetoric, the topic thought can be located anywhere in a paragraph. Most commonly, however, it appears either at the beginning or at the end, where it attracts the most attention. Sometimes it appears at the end as a summary statement of the topic thought expressed earlier. Sometimes the construction of a paragraph—such as a paragraph in which a point is being made deductively—dictates that the topic thought appear at the end. In most paragraphs, however, the topic thought appears at or near the beginning.

Writers of fiction do not have to worry about the strategic location of the topic sentence. People who read novels and short stories do so out of choice, not out of necessity. Consequently, writers can expect that most readers will read the book or magazine fairly carefully and comprehensively. Therefore, wherever the topic sentence is located, it will be read.

Readers of business and technical reports, however, usually read reports out of necessity, not choice. Consequently, they frequently try to skim through them as quickly as possible. In so doing, they often glance only at the first one or two sentences in each paragraph. In effect, they construct their own precis of the report, which is essentially the detailed outline with which the writer began.

To make certain that your main idea in each paragraph is read, therefore, it is a good idea to express it at the beginning of the paragraph whenever it is appropriate to do so. In that way, it will attract the attention of even the reader who skims.

COMPLETENESS

When you were in school and the teacher assigned you a paragraph or two to write, the first question you probably asked was, "How long should it be?" Teachers themselves are frequently responsible for this emphasis on arithmetic instead of on composition. They frequently include a numerical constraint as part of their assignment: "Write two paragraphs of 50 words each," or "Write a paragraph of six sentences."

Although experience has shown that readers of technical and business reports grasp most easily material presented in units of from 75 to 200 words, this is more an average than a norm. The length of paragraphs cannot be legislated. It depends on the complexity of the idea and on the reader's familiarity with the subject. In general, a paragraph should not end until the topic thought has been adequately discussed.

How can you tell whether you have adequately developed the topic idea? Intuition? Telepathy? Assumption? Gut feeling? None of these. There is a much more reliable guideline. Each topic idea contains key terms that must be addressed in the development. If all of the key terms are not addressed, portions of the topic thought have been neglected.

Consider, for example, the topic thought, "A solution to the energy crisis will depend more on conservation than on new technology." The key terms are *solution, energy crisis, conservation,* and *new technology.* Each of the following three paragraphs is an attempt to develop that topic idea. Note that the first attempt is inadequate because it simply repeats the topic thought in paraphrases and hence does not advance the idea:

> A solution to the energy crisis will depend more on conservation than on new technology. If we are to find a way out of the energy shortage, we must use our resources more wisely. We cannot depend on scientists to solve the problem through technological development.

Note that the second attempt is also unsatisfactory. It fails to develop the concept expressed in the topic thought because it introduces irrelevant ideas without comment. Thus, the paragraph is much like the earlier example dealing with Writing Skills, in which the bases for several paragraphs are crammed into one geometrical design.

> A solution to the energy crisis will depend more on conservation than on new technology. Conservationist organizations are beginning to focus their attention on our use of energy as well as the preservation of our natural resources and wildlife. The contribution of the scientific community, on the other hand, appears to be limited to calculating the moment when we will run out of fuel.

Note that the third attempt, however, addresses the key terms and is therefore an adequate development.

> A solution to the energy crisis will depend more on conservation than on new technology. Over the next decade, our scientists will probably develop new sources of energy such as solar, geothermal, and nuclear. These sources, however, are limited for a number of reasons. Nuclear energy, for example, is limited by both the radiation hazard and the relatively small supplies of uranium; and solar and geothermal energy are limited by the number of locations in which they can be applied. In total, therefore, they will increase our energy resources by only 10 to 20 percent. Conservation, on the other hand, could extend the life of our present resources by 50 to 100 percent. For example, by lowering the thermostats in our homes and offices, we can reduce our consumption of fuel by 25 to 30 percent; by adhering to lower speed limits, we can realize similar savings in gasoline consumption; and by minimizing the use of air conditioners and fans, we can cut our consumption of electricity by 10 to 15 percent. In short, if we want to solve the energy crisis, we will have to find the most energy-conserving technique to satisfy energy-consuming requirements.

Remember, then, that the topic sentence contains the seeds of its own development. Look for the term(s). Make sure each term is addressed in the development.

It is not necessary to develop key terms in the sequence in which they appear in the topic sentence. In fact, the logic of the development might preclude your treating them in the sequence in which they were introduced in the topic idea. It is the relationship of the terms rather than their sequence that dictates the order in which you choose to discuss them. For example, in the development of the topic statement "The great enemy of communication is the illusion of it," the key terms are *enemy, communication,* and *illusion;* yet the logic of the development suggests that *communication* and *illusion* be defined and the difference noted as a prelude to demonstrating how one is the *enemy* of the other. Consequently, the order of development would be *communication, illusion,* and *enemy.*

When writers have difficulty developing paragraphs, one of two causes is usually responsible: (1) failure to expand expandable ideas and (2) an attempt to expand unexpandable details.

In the first instance, the writer inadvertently ignores a well-conceived topic idea. Instead of adding detail, the attempt at development in reality ignores the topic thought and adds opinion and suggestion. Such paragraphs usually lack not only proper development but also organic unity:

> Automotive repairs can be expensive and inconvenient. Don't let mechanics or service managers talk you into unneeded repairs. Insisting on a written estimate of parts and labor is a good idea.

In the second instance, the writer selects as his topic idea a thought too small to form the basis of a paragraph. Very simply, he fails to distinguish between a statement that requires evidence or qualification (such as an opinion, a judgment, a recommendation) and one that does not (such as a specific detail). The former are broad, encompassing concepts or ideas, whereas the latter are narrowly restrictive. For example, "Government regulations are strangling business" is a broad, evaluative statement requiring supporting detail to make it clear and acceptable, whereas "The company is located in Lowell, Mass." is a factual detail that requires no additional explanation to be understood or accepted.

Thus, when a writer begins a paragraph with a narrow factual detail, he frequently paints himself into a corner. Anything he adds in an attempt at developing that idea will be either redundant or extraneous. In trying to work his way out, he may add evaluative statements and suggestions that do not develop the first statement but that need development themselves. The result is the same as that illustrated in the paragraph above:

> Today people are paying more than 11 percent for home mortgages. It is ridiculous to pay such a high rate. Until interest rates on mortgages are reduced, people should refuse to purchase real estate.

Although factual details are required to support broad statements, they are not needed as evidence for each other. Each is thus, in a sense, self-sufficient. Because factual details are sometimes closely related, however, one may appear to expand on the other when in reality the two in combination merely enlarge a topic idea that is not expressed.

Consider, for example, this statement:

The company employs 2,000 people.

In a one-sentence paragraph, that factual detail as the topic sentence poses no problem. If a writer attempts to develop that statement, however, he has a problem. He may think he is developing it, for example, by adding a second thought:

The company employs 2,000 people. Of these, 60 percent are classified as professional staff and 40 percent as support staff.

In effect, however, he has merely created a fractionated idea. Moreover, the total number of employees becomes incidental to the percentages. In the combination of the two sentences, the complete idea emerges: "Of the company's 2,000 employees, 60 percent are professional staff and 40 percent are support staff."

The point is that as long as specific facts stated in individual sentences can be more concisely presented in a single sentence, all that you have accomplished in effect—regardless of the number of sentences you have used—is simply to create a one-sentence statement of specific detail that is not expandable rather than a topic thought that can be expanded.

Even if your paragraph is a collection of specific details that support an unexpressed topic idea, you should remember two important things. First, be sure you recognize that you are expanding an implied topic sentence and not the first sentence of the paragraph. Second, remember that to supply the implied topic thought, the reader is going to have to read the entire paragraph and relate all the facts accurately. The reader who skims may therefore be misled by your first sentence. Consider, for example, this paragraph:

The company was founded in 1921. It has had only two presidents: the founder and his son. Both have provided an essential ingredient of success—excellent management. In its first year of operation, the company employed only 15 people; sales totalled $200,000. Today, with a highly respected name, the company employs 2,000 people, and sales have reached $150 million.

The implied topic thought may have been "The company has had a long history of success," but the reader who skims might not perceive that intended focus. Reading only the first sentence, he might pass that fact off as unimportant; reading the first two, he might conclude that it is a tightly held family business. That is why it is better to express topic ideas in business and technical writing. Stating them protects against blunted perception and unwarranted deductive or inductive conclusions.

METHODS OF DEVELOPMENT

When a writer develops a paragraph, he should have a purpose in doing so. It may be simply to review a familiar concept or idea; it may be to explain a complex idea or to clarify one not thoroughly understood; it may be to re-examine a concept or to re-enforce it; it may be to stimulate additional consideration of an idea; or it may be to replace an old perception with a new one. It is his objective, therefore, coupled with his assessment of the complexity of the thought and the reader's familiarity with the subject, that helps the writer select an appropriate method of development.

A number of methods, which can be used alone or in combination, are available to the writer. One of the most common is example. When you are explaining a thought or concept, an example helps the reader to relate the unfamiliar to the familiar or to envision in concrete detail what might otherwise remain a fuzzy abstraction. The following paragraph is developed by examples.

Jargon assumes many forms. In one form, it consists of simple abbreviations such as ETD, LSD, EKG, and PVC. In another form, it appears as expanded and pronounceable abbreviations (called acronyms) such as laser, Fortran, scuba, and radar. In still another form, it is composed of special meanings assigned to conventional terms by those in various trades and professions; for example, market analysts speak of softness and saturation, those in computer technology talk of patches, and space engineers talk of umbilicals. Finally, new words coined to keep pace with new concepts create a common form of jargon; for example, the space program gave us ullage, our concern about environmental pollution gave us biodegradable, and our sociological considerations gave us exurbanite.

Another common method is analogy, which is merely an extended example.

A bat is able to detect objects much like a radar system. A bat gives off a very high-pitched sound that strikes an object and is reflected back to the bat's hearing sensors. These sensors determine the direction from which the sound comes and how far away the object is. Similarly, a radar system sends out pulses of energy that also strike an object and are reflected back to radar sensors. The sensors determine the direction and distance of the object.

In many instances, the specific detail provided as part of the development closely resembles example:

> Digital computers are being used today in areas that even their most stalwart supporters didn't dream of a decade or so ago. Most expected them to be used in science and technology. Few, however, expected them to be used for making airline reservations, for billing meals and lodging, and for making purchases in department stores. Even fewer expected them to be used by the IRS to check tax returns; by the graphic-arts industry to set type, draw line charts, and check spelling; and by state and local police departments to control traffic.

When the purpose of the development is to provide a quick review, historical summary or chronology can be used as the basis of the development. Here is how historical summary might appear:

> Data processing was introduced at PRC in 1967. The system was designed to enter data by means of punched cards and to handle the requirements of only one plant. As the requirements of additional plants were added, however, the 150 percent increase in processing overtaxed the card-oriented system. Therefore a new and more sophisticated system was installed in 1976.

Here is how chronology might be used:

> Every company passes through a four-stage life cycle. In the first, or embryonic, stage the company emphasizes product development and sales. The organization is loose and flexible, and the leadership must be entrepreneurial. In the second, or growth, stage the structure is less flexible, and the leadership adopts the stance of a market manager. In the third, or mature, stage the structure becomes rigid, and the leadership must administer a business that has reached a plateau. In the final, or aging, stage sales and profits begin to decline and management "milks" the business.

Superficially at least, chronological development seems similar to enumeration. The difference, of course, is that enumeration is only accidentally time-associated, whereas the chronological development is generically time-related. The following paragraph typifies enumeration.

> There are two corollaries to this question of detail. First, you should omit anything that has no bearing on your central theme. Extraneous material distracts an audience. Second, key ideas should be repeated. Repetition in an oral presentation offers the listener an opportunity to review a fact, to catch up with a fact, or to consider a fact from a slightly different point of view.

Another common method of developing a paragraph is to provide reasons. This method can be employed whether you are providing information or trying to persuade.

> In making an oral presentation, be careful about including too much detail. The typical audience cannot assimilate in 20 to 30 minutes every detail of a project that may have taken months to complete. Nor is there any need for an audience to be supplied with all sorts of minutiae in order to understand the major ideas. Facts of marginal contribution may only cloud or confuse the issue. Therefore, give your audience only enough detail to make your point clear.

In developing a paragraph by an appeal to logic, writers often resort to methods involving deduction, induction, or cause and effect. Here is an example of development through cause and effect.

> The weakness of the plan soon became apparent. Prices rose excessively; production in areas not controlled by the agreement increased; and new channels of supply developed. As the price rose, competitors developed a synthetic product. As competition from synthetic producers grew, management admitted the plan was not accomplishing what it was intended to.

Another common method of developing paragraphs is comparison or contrast. Comparison or contrast may be used to develop a single paragraph or several successive paragraphs, depending on the extent of the similarities or differences being discussed. Here is an example.

> There are two philosophies of medicine: the primitive or superstitious, and the modern or rational. They are in complete opposition. The former involves the belief that disease is caused by supernatural forces. It associates disease with certain forms of evil and attempts to control it by ceremonial and superstitious measures. On the other hand, rational medicine is based on the concept that disease arises from natural causes. In this view, disease is viewed as the result of a violation of sanitary laws rather than as a violation of moral laws. Modern medicine tries to prevent and cure disease on the basis of scientific investigation and approaches proved to be effective by experience.

On many occasions, a number of methods are used in combination in the development of a paragraph. For example, definition is frequently used in conjunction with example, and deduction is used in conjunction with providing reasons. As with so many other facets of effective writing, the type and number used in combination vary with the author's objective, the nature of the subject, and the reader's background and biases.

COHERENCE

Each sentence in a paragraph is a distinct syntactical unit containing an independent and complete thought. If each sentence is to play its proper role in the development of the topic thought, however, it must help to advance the thought; it must be part of a synthesis; it must provide continuity; it must be related to other sentences in the sequence.

Fundamental to establishing proper relationships is logical progression. Even though the individual thoughts may be expressed clearly and simply, the overall idea and purpose of the paragraph may not be clearly and easily understood if the ideas seem strewn haphazardly throughout the paragraph. Consider, for example, the original version of the paragraph below, which was the opening paragraph of a memorandum. Note how in the revised version, the sentences remain intact; only the sequence has been altered.

Original	Revised
Clarification of the use of our bank-wide copying and printing facilities appears appropriate at this time. Some departments are unaware of equipment that is available and how and when to use it. Before the major moves of last year, a great deal of time was spent on this entire subject. The decision was made to purchase new machinery for our Printing Department and to decentralize office copying.	Before the major moves of last year, we decided to purchase new equipment for our Printing Department and to decentralize office copying. Now, however, some departments are unaware of the equipment that is available and how and when to use it. Therefore, clarification of the use of our bank-wide copying and printing facilities appears to be appropriate at this time.

Coherence also involves more obvious linkage. This linkage includes syntactic patterns, transitional elements, and repetition. Note how the pronouns in the following example point forward and backward. For example, the pronoun *its* in the first sentence points ahead to its referent *Oakview Airport* and thus connects the first portion of the sentence with the rest of the sentence. Similarly, the words *some, others,* and *all* connect the sentences in which they appear to previous sentences.

In its 25-year history, Oakview Airport has served the leading airlines. Some are international carriers; others operate only within the United States. All carry passengers exclusively.

Pronouns provide coherence in other ways. In the following paragraph, for example, note how the repetition of the pronouns *you* and *they* provide syntactical logic and consistency in establishing a perspective.

> You engineers, scientists, economists, and others who write technical reports and papers are a much maligned group. Editors insult you, reviewers ridicule you, readers slander you, professional writers disown you, and English teachers abhor you. They charge that you do not know how to write. The extremists among them contend that you have perpetrated more atrocities with words than Genghis Khan did with swords. The moderates suggest the atrocities are about even. Therefore, it is time that someone set your writing in proper perspective to dispel the ignorance and illogic in which this criticism is rooted.

Repetition of words and phrases is a common means of linking sentences. In the following paragraph, note how the sentences provide continuity by the repetition of key words from previous sentences.

> The following assignments cover all the writing problems discussed in this chapter. In almost every assignment a list of possible subjects is provided. These lists call for comment. Some of the subjects may impress you as not being especially technical, but there are valid reasons for their inclusion. It would be impossible to suggest several highly technical subjects in every conceivable field of specialization. Therefore, a good many subjects have been included that can be handled without specialized knowledge.

Transitional words and phrases are often used to establish coherence. They frequently indicate a change in rank or direction of a thought and thus make it easier to follow and understand. Some of the more common types of transitions are listed below.

Transitional Element	What Is Signified
Furthermore, moreover, in addition, first, second, third, finally	Adding detail
Therefore, as a result, thus, because, consequently, hence	Causality
Similarly, in like manner, likewise, still, here again, compared with	Comparison
Conversely, whereas, nevertheless, by contrast, however, on the other hand, but, yet	Contrast

While, formerly, after, when, meanwhile	Time sequence
Although, if	Condition
Whether, either, or	Options
For instance, for example, in this case	Illustration
Indeed, in fact	Intensification
That is, in other words	Repetition
In summary, in brief, in short, to sum up	Summary

Transitional words and phrases are much like condiments: we are often aware not so much of their presence as of their absence. Note how the transitional expressions, which are in parentheses in the paragraph below, make the paragraph easier to read and understand because they clarify relationships between thoughts. If you are skeptical of the value of transitional phrases and words, try reading the paragraph below after omitting the words in parentheses and beginning new sentences at each underscore.

Certain considerations may prevent Hallowell Company from entering the market for widgets. (First), (although) the company is not convinced that its already overburdened sales force could handle the additional work, it does not want to expand its sales staff (because) sales costs are already quite high. (Second), its R&D staff may not be able to devote adequate time to work on widgets. Recently the department was seriously affected (when) six senior members left the company. (Consequently), further work on new products is unlikely.

Merely supplying transitions or purposeful repetition or any other form of verbal bridge is not a panacea. Unity and coherence go hand in hand. When relevant ideas are arranged in logical sequence, easy transitions are enhanced. When ideas are irrelevant or the sequence is faulty, however, the mere insertion of connectives will not solve the problem. For example, in the original version of the paragraph following, the coherence is impaired because the author selected the wrong topic sentence in view of the facts presented in subsequent sentences. Given a topic thought that imparts a pervasive relevance to the remaining sentences, logical arrangement and helpful transitions produce a clear and effective paragraph in the revised version.

Original	Revised
For almost a decade there has been a concerted effort to improve emergency medical care in the United States, and substantial progress is now being made in many places. Accidents are the leading cause of death in this country for people from ages 1 to 37 and in the fourth place for all ages. Of the 115,000 accidental deaths each year, an estimated 18,000 could be prevented if the victim were treated correctly within minutes of the emergency. In addition, 350,000 victims of cardiac arrest could be saved with immediate care.	Many people in the United States die needlessly, because proper emergency medical care is not available. For example, an estimated 18,000 of the 115,000 accidental deaths each year could be prevented if the victim were treated correctly within minutes of the emergency. In addition, 350,000 victims of cardiac arrest could be saved with immediate care. Now, however, after about a decade of concerted effort, substantial progress is being made in many places.

EMPHASIS

Emphasis is essentially a product of unity and coherence, in that it is governed by the selection and arrangement of detail. Note the difference in emphasis in the two versions of the following letter.

ORIGINAL

Several years ago, our wholly owned subsidiary purchased a modern hot-blast cupola facility to develop a process to extract metal values from a unique slag. The research was unsuccessful and the plant turned to the production of high-quality pig iron produced from number 2 scrap bundles. Unfortunately, we have not been able to sell more than 20 percent of the plant's output, largely because of competition from foreign pig, and this level of operation is not adequate to achieve profitable operating conditions. This situation, in combination with the fact that our corporate goals in the past year have been diverted substantially from the metallurgical field, prompts us to offer this operation for sale. A brief description of the subject facilities and plant is attached to this letter.

The cupola is the most unique part of this plant since it is of the modern, hot-blast, water-cooled design with complete air-pollution control equipment. The cupola is capable of operating with a reducing atmosphere and employing scrap silicon carbide rather than ferro-silicon as a silicon charge. Essentially, the furnace is midway between a normal cupola and a blast furnace in its operating capabilities. These characteristics result in production costs ($41/net ton), which are quite outstanding for a cupola of its size, and these costs have been verified by an independent consulting firm. Their analysis is available for your perusal.

This facility can be a valuable asset for an organization such as yours if you have a requirement or market for an inexpensive source of hot foundry metal or pig iron. At the moment, the plant is shut down for major refractory maintenance but it is available for inspection.

I invite you to telephone me if you are interested in obtaining further information regarding our intentions or wish to visit the facilities.

REVISION

Because of a substantial change in our corporate goals, we are offering for sale a modern hot-blast cupola that can manufacture 150,000 tons per year of high quality pig iron or hot foundry metals at a production cost of $41 per net ton.

If you have a requirement or market for an inexpensive source of these materials, you will find this facility a valuable asset. The operating capabilities of the cupola are midway between those of a normal cupola and a blast furnace. It is water-cooled, has complete air-pollution control equipment, can operate with a reducing atmosphere, and employs scrap silicon carbide, rather than ferro-silicon, as a silicon charge.

At the moment, the plant is shut down for routine refractory maintenance, but it is available for your inspection. If you would like to visit the facilities or obtain further information about them, please telephone me.

The interesting aspect of the letters is that in neither one was the writer attempting to convey that the problem was attributable to technical difficulty. The problem was that the parent corporation was not experienced in the market for the product that the hot-blast facility was oriented toward. Consequently, it had difficulty marketing the product. Therefore, the company decided to sell the facility. The letter was intended to evoke interest from potential buyers. Clearly, the original version does not.

The reason the original version fails in its intent is that a great deal of irrelevant detail is included. Moreover, negative aspects are placed in positions of importance. By contrast, the revised version includes only relevant information and puts up in the front those details that are of greatest importance to the reader. Hence the difference. Selection and arrangement of detail vitally affect emphasis.

In selecting and arranging detail, you can use at least three rhetorical techniques: mass or proportion, position, and repetition.

When mass or proportion is used, each item in the topic thought is discussed at a length appropriate to its importance. Normally, therefore, the more important the topic, the lengthier the discussion.

Position can be used by itself or in conjunction with mass or proportion to create emphasis. Since the positions of greatest emphasis are the beginning and the end, important ideas are frequently placed in one or both of these positions. When both positions are used, the topic idea is often expressed at the beginning and paraphrased at the end for re-enforcement.

Position and purposeful repetition can serve as complements. But repetition can be used in other ways as well. Note the effectiveness of the repetition of the term *management* in the following paragraph. It not only creates emphasis but provides continuity as well.

> Management makes the successful organization. Effective management earns a profit even in this day of the "profit squeeze." Progressive management learns to solve the complex problems of the twentieth century. Successful, effective, progressive management is the theme of the American Management Association.

FUNCTIONS OF PARAGRAPHS

Paragraphs are designed to present information in digestible and palatable increments. To do this, they are used in a variety of ways: to introduce subjects or topics, to provide transitions, to amplify, to summarize. Here, for example, is how paragraphs are used to introduce a subject.

> Every day we spend an average of 35 percent of our time communicating by speaking. In business, government, and education, for example, speech is used in conversations, counselling sessions,

interviews, meetings, sales campaigns, planning sessions, and training programs. Each of these activities is a presentation, in that its basic purpose is to acquaint an audience with information, often with the intent of aiding in or influencing a decision.

Depending on the circumstances, presentations can be impromptu, read from a prepared text, memorized, or given extemporaneously. The advantages and disadvantages of each type are discussed in the following sections.

On other occasions, paragraphs are used to create transitions. Note how in the example below, the second paragraph creates a transition from the problems cited in the first paragraph to the solutions suggested in the third.

All of us, at one time or another, have had difficulty keeping our eyes open during a lecture, a sales presentation, a conference, or a seminar. And our heavy-lidded reaction is not always caused by the speaker or the subject matter. We are simply victims of fatigue. Sometimes we come to a morning conference without getting enough sleep; sometimes we attend an afternoon meeting after eating a big lunch; sometimes we attend evening classes after a day of mental or physical exertion. Although fatigue is the root of the difficulty, our tendency to relax under certain circumstances or in certain surroundings quickens the process. For example, we find a comfortable seat in a lecture hall, the temperature in the room is conducive to drowsiness, or the room is darkened while slides, overhead projections, or movies are used as visual aids.

Our drowsiness, of course, is not only wasteful but also always discourteous and sometimes distracting. We not only fail to assimilate the information being presented, but also prevent others from listening effectively by attracting their attention at least intermittently.

We can help to overcome the difficulty in several ways. First, we should get enough sleep. Although an occasional emergency may prevent us from getting enough sleep, most of us stay up late of our own accord. Second, if the heat in the room is posing a problem, we should ask to have it turned down. Third, we should take notes; by keeping occupied, we remain alert. Fourth, we should not select a seat that is too comfortable. Finally, we should try to arrange our schedule so that we attend presentations during those periods when our communication efficiency is normally greatest.

Paragraphs used to amplify are perhaps the most common. Most of the paragraphs shown as examples in this chapter are designed to amplify. In fact, the third paragraph in the example above illustrates an amplifying paragraph.

Finally, a summarizing paragraph is used to recapitulate important ideas in a detailed discussion of a topic.

> In summary, the use of summarizing topic sentences focuses the writer's and reader's attention on the immediate subject. They help to organize sentences into paragraphs and paragraphs into sections. As an expansion of an outline, such sentences provide a basis for better, shorter, and more useful reports that are approved more quickly.

EXERCISES

1. Evaluate the following paragraphs.

   a. The energy crisis has brought along with it a multitude of problems for a wide variety of industries and businesses. Many have never before had to consider long-term planning for fear of supply interruption and plant shutdown. In addition, regulators in the United States at various levels of government find themselves heavily involved in the development of policy that will minimize the impact of the growing energy shortage in the United States.

   b. Play the role of devil's advocate with caution, since it sometimes creates more problems than it solves. This consists of deliberately taking a position different from the one taken by the subordinate to provoke him into a defense of his position or conviction. The statement should not be highly critical or personal. The goal is to get the subordinate talking enough to break the ice.

   c. Price and wage control is an effective means of retarding inflation and stabilizing the economy. The relationship between prices and wages is so intimate that the slightest variation in one will inevitably be reflected in the other. For example, a $100 increase in the cost of automobiles will result in the need for a $100 salary increase if the general public is to continue buying cars and at the same time maintain the present standard of living. In order to control this "snowball" effect (in other words, inflation), what is required is a government body whose responsibility is the regulation of prices and wages. This type of agency would undoubtedly suffer, however, from all of the bureaucratic problems. However, the net effects, a reduction in inflation and a stable economy, would certainly benefit the public.

d. The effectiveness of the Orientation Program depends largely on two main factors: how the presentation of the program is done, and on the ability of the participant to absorb the presented material. It seems to me that not all departments gave their employees enough time to prepare for the presentation of their functions. This could have resulted from the fact that a large number of the employees were on vacation. So a different scheduling approach should be adopted. The time allocated for the Orientation Program should be spread out. This would result in a more flexible scheduling, and also it would give a chance to the employee participating in the tour to gather more information about the departments to be visited. I found helpful the use of printed material (organization charts, text of special contracts, etc.) in the understanding of the presentation.

e. The strongest impression created by the survey of new product development was that it's difficult to know who is winning the game if no one is keeping score. We had assumed that the divisions maintained reasonably systematic records of work progress, costs, time requirements, and the results of new product development. We found, however, that all but two did not. As a result, we had to delay our analysis while the divisions tried to pull together information from memory and from various files. Moreover, when this information was finally supplied, no one could vouch for its accuracy or completeness. Our analysis, therefore, reflects these shortcomings.

f. The complete processing cycle requires our section to draw services from three centers—the keypunch section, the computer section, and the switchboard section. We have always received excellent cooperation and service from each center. We feel obliged in turn not to interfere with their ability to handle all subscribers in sequence. This situation can lead to minor delays in our processing.

2. Indicate whether each of the following ideas represents a good, marginal, or poor topic sentence.

a. The payroll was computerized in 1971.

b. San Francisco is changing.

c. An acronym is a pronounceable abbreviation of a compound term.

d. An effective paragraph has three attributes: unity, coherence, and emphasis.

e. Dr. Barry was thirty-four years old when he was appointed director of research.

f. Sales in 1978 declined 22 percent from 1977.

g. The company has been in business for 50 years.

h. Following a loan reduction to $160,000 in 1970, our credit began its rise to its current level.

3. Place the following sentences in their proper sequence.

(1) Depending on the costs estimated from the pilot study and the demand potential from the market study, it might either abandon the project, build a large plant, or build a small one. (2) Rather, decisions are made in stages. (3) If the survey results are favorable, it might spend $500,000 on a pilot plant to investigate production methods. (4) Thus, the final decision is actually made in stages, with subsequent decisions depending on the results of previous decision. (5) Most important decisions are not made once-and-for-all at one time. (6) It might spend $100,000 for a survey of supply-demand conditions in the agricultural chemical industry. (7) For example, a petroleum firm considering the possibility of expanding into agricultural chemicals might take a series of steps.

4. Select from among the following sentences those that are relevant, and place them in the proper sequence.

(1) The extremists among them contend that you have perpetrated more atrocities with words than Genghis Khan with swords; the moderates suggest that the atrocities are about even. (2) Those who claim the technical style is unimaginative are ignorant of the philosophy and motives that have fostered it. (3) Therefore, it's time that someone set your writing in proper perspective to dispel the ignorance and illogic in which this criticism is rooted. (4) You engineers, scientists, economists, and others who write technical reports and papers are a much maligned group. (5) Those who say your writing is ineffective overlook its tremendous psychological value. (6) They have repeated these charges with enough consistency and conviction to threaten your confidence and possibly destroy a revolutionary literary genre. (7) Even those who are not totally successful in camouflaging a thought can be commended for a gallant effort. (8) They charge that you don't know how to write. (9) Editors insult you, reviewers ridicule you, readers slander you, professional writers disown you, and English teachers abhor you. (10) Reconciling these two apparanetly conflicting motives would be a very difficult problem for the unimaginative.

5. How can this sequence of paragraphs be improved?

Two temporary but substantial impediments exist to the successful adoption of automated composition systems by traditional and in-plant publishing organizations. First, the wide diversity of products, while contributing to a rapid evolution of systems, has also produced confusion in the market. No supplier holds a commanding position, and each promulgates its own standards. Thus, phototypesetters all use different codes, copy-processing systems call for complex and often special interfaces, and editing terminals are designed to operate only with other systems of the same manufacturer. The teletypesetter (TTS) code has survived—despite its inefficiency—because it is the lowest common denominator. Under competitive pressures, suppliers have added to the confusion by announcing products before they have been tested, sometimes before they have been built, and nearly always long before they have become available for shipment. Buyers have become frequently confused as suppliers have offered suprisingly little technical information.

We believe this problem will be ameliorated, in part because there will be fewer suppliers in the marketplace in three years. In the wake of this confusion, we foresee many systems performing at marginal levels. These will have to be substantially changed or replaced if users are to implement new automated composition applications successfully.

The second major problem is that new systems call for new skills, new organizations, and new management practices. The reaction of trade compositors has evolved from resistance to genuine interest. Some new organization patterns have emerged already, and others will. "Assistant Managing Editor for Production," for example, identifies the newsroom systems manager at a major newspaper; "Vice-President for Communications" (or "for Information Systems") is a corporate assignment that increasingly encompasses automated composition and business information systems along with other responsibilities, including data processing, library functions, public relations, and word processing. Still, for most users, the organization and management of automated composition resources has been a difficult issue to resolve, and installations have suffered from the parochial interests of the production department or the more experimental, often hardware-oriented attitude of the data processing department. Nonetheless, we are optimistic that these problems will gradually be overcome and over the long run will not hamper the shipment growth trend and a profitable evolution of systems for a broad variety of users.

6
Editing the Draft: Applying the Finish

Unless you are one of the gifted few who can commit to paper in a single effort thoughts that are remarkably well organized, compellingly clear, factually complete, and stylistically flawless, you will need to review and revise your draft. The question, then, is not should the draft be edited, but rather when and how much. Several considerations govern the answer: the nature of the subject, the way the information is to be used, the significance of the information, and whether time is critical.

In deciding when to edit your draft, you have three options. You can edit as you write, immediately after you have finished writing, or after you have put the draft aside for several days.

Writing and editing simultaneously is not a good idea unless you are writing a short letter or memo about a subject that is simple and straightforward. For example, if you must submit each week the number of units produced or in inventory as a matter of routine information, you might choose to edit as you write if, indeed, any editing is required.

Editing immediately after you have finished writing might be appropriate if you are writing a report in which the immediacy of the response is as important as the effectiveness of the presentation. For example, many times people in business are asked at three o'clock to have a report prepared by four or five o'clock. In fact, even when the deadline is not that stringent, the recency of the data may be as important as the clarity of the prose. For example, if you are asked to provide a forecast, it is obviously useless to spend so much time editing the report that projection becomes history.

Ideally, of course, editing is more effective when you allow a cooling period. In a memo or letter, you may have reacted emotionally to an issue. The cooling off period will allow you to view the issue dispassionately and revise your response accordingly. Even when you have written objectively and dispassionately, the cooling period provides enough time to neutralize the effects of the paternalistic attitude many authors develop toward their prose. Paternalism tends to produce editorial blindness. By putting the draft aside for a few days, you won't rely so heavily on memory and read into the draft what you intended to say rather than what you actually said.

In deciding how much editing is needed, read the draft through carefully and measure it against the standards you have established to meet your reader's needs. Ask yourself such questions as:

Is the question or problem clearly stated?

Is the answer or solution stated in the conclusion(s) or recommendation(s)?

Does the report provide enough evidence in support of the conclusion(s) or recommendation(s)?

Is all of the information relevant?

Is the data timely, accurate, and well interpreted?

Is the data presented in an appropriate form (table, text, graph)?

Are the important points brought out clearly and concisely?

Are all special terms explained fully?

Is the report easy to read?

Perfection in substance and in the communication of it is always the goal of editing. That is why if you can control the schedule for preparing the report, it is important to allow enough time for a thorough editing job. If you cannot control the schedule, you will have to be selective in your editing in the light of your priorities. Ideally, your editing should cover a whole range of considerations: completeness, accuracy, clarity, conciseness, correctness, tone, pace, consistency, and stylistic considerations. Some of these considerations, however, are more important than others. Accuracy and clarity, for example, are more important than consistency and convention. Therefore, make certain that when time constraints force you to be selective in your editing, you consider the need for revision in terms of your reader's priorities as well as your objectives.

In evaluating and revising your draft, you may find the following guidelines helpful.

COMPLETENESS

Completeness means simply that you have provided the reader with enough detail in view of his needs and his background. Remember that any description, any explanation, any concept can only be expressed by the writer and understood by the reader in the context of the experience of each. And when each has not shared the same experience or has not the same background, the message may not be completely understood.

When the writer and reader do not share the same experience, the communication of an idea appears as shown in Figure 1.

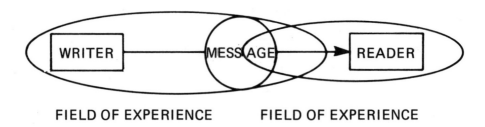

FIELD OF EXPERIENCE   FIELD OF EXPERIENCE

Figure 1   Message Incompletely Communicated

In such instances, only the portion of the message overlapped by each person's field of experience is communicated. The rest of the message is highly susceptible to misunderstanding or nonunderstanding.

The purpose of evaluating a report for completeness, therefore, is to make certain that the entire message is circumscribed by the experience of both parties, as shown in Figure 2.

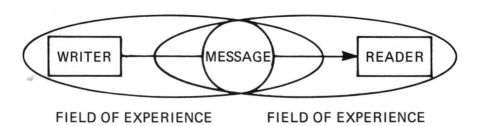

FIELD OF EXPERIENCE   FIELD OF EXPERIENCE

Figure 2   Message Completely Communicated

You can expand the reader's field of experience by adding detail. One way is to provide needed background information. It may be the explanation of a method you employed, the definition of a market, the history of a problem, or the discussion of the reliability of data. You may choose to devote an entire section to this kind of information, or you may choose merely to include it as an introductory paragraph or two within the sections in which the supporting detail is discussed.

A second way is to define special terms in simpler terms, in paraphrases, or by examples. If, for example, you were writing to a highly knowledgeable audience, you could say:

> It is possible for two structures to be homeomorphic.

To an audience that is less technical, you might add this explanation:

> It is possible for two structures to be homeomorphic; that is, to have mathematically equivalent surfaces.

To an audience with little or no knowledge of the subject, you might phrase it this way:

> It is possible for two structures to be homeomorphic; that is, for one structure, theoretically at least, to be able to be twisted or pressed into the shape of the other. For example, given enough pressure, a football can theoretically assume the shape of a small basketball.

The important thing to remember is that the explanation should be geared to the audience's experience. Too many writers offer an explanation that merely adds to the reader's difficulty. For example, one educator informed the parents that their child was having a problem:

> She is falling behind in her MLO (Manipulative Learning Operation).

As it turned out, she was having difficulty in laboratory work!

Completeness and clarity are inseparable. Therefore, in many instances the need for additional explanation is unnecessary if the author eliminates the use of needless jargon and its pretentious first cousin, Latinisms and other foreign phrases. For example,

> Price elasticities must be calculated first on a ceteris parabus basis.

The Latin phrase simply means "all other things being equal." Therefore, the author could easily have written:

In calculating price elasticities, we must first assume that all other things are equal.

Completeness in some instances requires the addition of detail. In others, however, it requires the omission of detail. When you do not provide enough detail, readers may accuse you of arrogance; when you provide needless detail—when you constantly write down to readers—they may accuse you of condescension. As E.B. White has said: ". . . no writer can improve his work until he discards the dulcet notion that the reader is feeble-minded, for writing is an act of faith, not a trick of grammar. Ascent is at the heart of the matter. . . ."* It is not necessary to treat readers as though they are high school dropouts. Treat them as intelligent and generally informed persons who have not explored the subject in perhaps the depth and from the perspective that you have. Just remember: your objective is to explain or propose something to the reader, not to prove that you are smarter than he is.

If you are writing to more than one reader and you recognize that some are familiar with all of the necessary terminology, whereas others may not be, include additional detail parenthetically if it is brief. A parenthetical expression signifies that the information is included only for those who need it. If the information is long enough to become an intrusion, put it in a footnote. In either case, let the reader decide whether he needs it or not. By so doing, you will come across as considerate rather than smug.

ACCURACY

Accuracy involves the logic of your argument as well as the precision of your calculations and the reliability of your sources. Consider, for example, the argument of an insurance executive who attempted to justify increased costs this way:

Whenever insurance companies are faced with the necessity of requesting increased rates to cover expenses, newspapers almost unanimously demand careful scrutiny of the requests. Yet these same newspapers impose rate increases without any public agency having any say in the matter. Whereas the rate increases of insurance companies have increased only 30 percent recently, newspapers have increased their prices 50 percent.

Although the percentages were accurate, the argument is specious

---

*E.B. White, "Calculating Machine," in *The Second Tree from the Corner,* Harper & Brothers, New York, 1951.

in two respects. First, the executive was talking about compulsory insurance, whereas the consumer is not compelled to buy a newspaper. Second, the percentages are grossly misleading, in that the 50 percent increase in newspapers involved a price jump of 5¢, whereas the 30 percent increase in insurance rates represented an average of $50 or more. Remember, statistics can be misleading if the reader is not apprised of the basis from which they are derived.

Similarly, in the light of the supporting statistics, consider the fallacy in the following observation.

Because of the lower percentage of college graduates in Bigtown, the educational levels of the main labor force are in general higher.

Years of School Completed	Percent of Labor Force
None	1.0
Elementary (1 - 8 years)	35.2
High School (1 - 3 years)	23.4
High School (4 years)	21.7
College (1 - 3 years)	9.5
College (4 years or more)	9.2
Median years completed	10.8

The percentages could be varied and produce the same effect. For example, if Elementary were 45.2 percent instead of 35.2, if High School (1 - 3 years) were 18.4 percent instead of 23.4 percent, and High School (4 years) were 16.7 percent instead of 21.7 percent, the levels of education would be lower than those shown in the table, while the percentage of college graduates would not have changed.

Undoubtedly the problem is in the use of the terms *higher* and *lower*. Since the author has provided no basis for comparison, the reader is left to supply his own.

Careless handling of statistics takes other forms. For example,

The governor has proposed a 1 percent increase in the state tax, from the current 3 percent to the suggested 4 percent.

Although it may be more palatable to the public presented in this way, such an increase represents 33⅓ percent. The writer should have more accurately said a 1 percentage point increase.

Nothing is more irritating to a reader than to be confronted with statistics that do not add properly. For example,

---

The population of the United States is projected to increase from 205.1 million in 1976 to 226.3 million in 1982. The breakdown by age groups is shown in Table 1.

U.S. Population Projection By Age Groupings
(Millions)

Age Group	1976	1982
Under 5	15.3	17.3
5 - 14	37.2	33.0
15 - 19	21.2	19.4
20 - 34	51.6	59.0
35 - 44	23.1	27.8
45 - 64	43.8	44.0
65 and above	22.9	25.8

According to the table, the population in 1976 was 215.1 million, in contradiction with the writer's stated 205.1 million. The reader is thus left wondering which figure is correct. If the table is incorrect, the reader may be skeptical about the projection because he has no way of knowing whether the error is in one age grouping or in several. Even if the table is correct, the reader cannot be sure. The conflicting totals will sow seeds of doubt and distrust.

The same type of inaccuracy is created in statements such as:

In the United States, only 6 percent of the population is employed in agriculture or related work, whereas 93 percent is employed in non-agricultural work.

Such a statement leaves the reader wondering whether one of the categories has been understated or whether a third category has been omitted.

On some occasions, writers imply an accuracy that does not exist. For example, in listing categories of information culled from a variety of sources, they copy the numbers as recorded. Thus, some sources may carry the data to three decimal points, whereas others may be rounded off. For the sake of balance, however, the writer may include the rounded-off number with a zero after the decimal point. By including the data in this form, the writer leads the reader to believe that the rounded-off numbers are just as precise as those carried to three decimal places.

Careless wording often causes inaccuracies. For example, consider this statement from a medical report.

> Blood samples were taken from 48 informed and consenting patients. The subjects ranged in age from 6 months to 22 years.

Or this statement, which suggests underground satellite movement.

> The satellite's initial period of revolution is 89 minutes. Its maximum distance from the center of the earth is 170 miles and the minimum 125 miles.

Remember that accuracy of information reflects the accuracy of your conclusion(s) or recommendation(s). Allowing fallacious argument or imprecise data to be disseminated in your report may cause your reader to question your competence not merely as a writer but also as an authoritative source.

CLARITY

Understanding is a prerequisite to sound judgment and decision. If the reader does not understand what you say, he is unable to take action. If he misinterprets what you say, he may take the wrong action. Clarity, therefore, is a prerequisite to effective communication.

Our first attempt at formulating ideas is not always precise, but because of the speed of our thoughts we do not always recognize their inadequacy. As we ponder our ideas, we may clothe them in vague, inept language either because we have not fully crystallized the idea or because we are not certain what we want to say. Sometimes in our haste to capture what we consider a worthwhile idea, we do not take the time to select and arrange our words carefully. Committed to paper, however, our thoughts are exposed. It is then that we get the opportunity to sort them out and correct them.

To revise them, of course, we must recognize the source of the difficulty. Here are some guidelines that cover the fundamental problems.

Use Specific Rather Than General Terms

Vague: I need the report within a reasonable time.

Specific: I need the report within two weeks.

Vague: The company's profits increased significantly.

Specific: The company's profits increased 25 percent.

Vague: Railroad service should be improved.

Specific: The railroad should provide cleaner coaches and ensure that trains depart and arrive on schedule.

Place Modifiers as Close As Possible to the Words They Modify

Ambiguous: Separatists pelted police guarding the government buildings with rocks and broken bottles.

Clear: Using rocks and broken bottles, separatists pelted the police guarding the government buildings.

Ambiguous: He was unaware that television sets contained so many components before he became a technician.

Clear: Before he became a technician, he was unaware that television sets contained so many components.

Ambiguous: Having arrived in Houston at 11 A.M., the afternoon was spent in visiting the Holmgren Company.

Clear: Having arrived in Houston at 11 A.M., I spent the afternoon visiting the Holmgren Company.

Ambiguous: Lacking management experience, we recommend the company acquire the necessary capability through a merger.

Clear: Lacking management experience, the company should acquire the necessary capability through a merger.

Make Sure Your References Are Clear

Vague: I have just been hired by a large industrial equipment manufacturer where I am responsible for the Public Relations Department, and I would appreciate very much if you could send me some information on the subject.

Clear: Having just been hired by the Public Relations Department of a large manufacturer of industrial equipment, I would appreciate your sending me information about competitive processes and consumer preferences relating to such equipment.

Vague: Although the employees believe the training program is beneficial, the supervisors feel they are not getting much out of it.

Clear: Although the employees believe the training is beneficial, the supervisors are not getting much out of it.

or

Although the employees believe the training is beneficial, the supervisors do not believe the employees are getting much out of it.

Vague: During the past two years, we made two major decisions regarding expansion: (1) not to expand in New England and (2) to build a new facility in the midwest. This proved to be unwise.

Clear: The decision not to expand in New England—one of two major decisions made during the past two years—proved to be unwise.

To Establish the Relative Importance of Ideas, Use Clauses Instead of Strings of Phrases

Poor: The unlikelihood of meeting orders from the majority of its customers is of concern to the bank due to the tardiness in the implementation of its new certificate-handling system.

Better: The bank is not sure it can meet all customer orders because its new certificate-handling system is not fully operational.

Poor: The inability to meet the increase in demand for its product due to insufficient equipment is a problem of major concern to the company.

Better: The company is greatly concerned that it cannot meet increased demand because it does not have enough equipment.

Insert Punctuation to Avoid Ambiguity

Poor: Resist the temptation to act hastily and think the move through.

Better: Resist the temptation to act hastily, and think the move through.

Poor: The Harris poll predicts that the candidate will get 283 electoral votes more than needed for election.

Better: The Harris poll predicts that the candidate will get 283 electoral votes, more than needed for election.

Use Simple Language

Pompous: He reacts negatively to aggressive stimulus.

Simplified: He lacks initiative.

Pompous: The co-existing systems of the rational manager and of discovered reality overlap and will always do so to the extent that the rational purposes of the manager coincide with the real interests of the people in the system. Equally important, when the two systems co-exist, they may be connected in the sense that they are more or less effective in modifying systems rationale, and the rational manager may be more or less effective in subjecting the real, informal social open system to acceptance of his system's rationale.

Simplified: A manager is most effective when he and his subordinates work toward common goals.

Pompous: A data base is a structured collection of data that is essentially nonredundant, providing a constant logical view of that data under a wide variety of physical realizations, thereby providing a high degree of data independence.

Simplified: A data base is a collection of essentially unrepeated items, all or a portion of which can be selected and arranged in a variety of relationships that meet the user's needs.

Pompous: Following an initial assessment of our data-gathering requirements, we will organize our data-gathering efforts in terms of our requirements.

Simplified: When we find out what we need, we'll go out and get it.

Break Complex Ideas Into Simpler Units

Poor: Sensors for measuring fluid flow are usually based on the measurement of an actual volume, such as home gas meters, or a variable head due to a differential in pressure, such as the orifice and venturi, variable area meters of which the most common type is the rotameter, velocity and current meters utilizing rotating elements, induced voltages, magnetic resonance and heat transfer, while mass meters designed to measure mass flow rather than volume flow or velocity are less commonly used.

Better: Sensors measure fluid flow in terms of volume or mass. The most commonly used are those based on volume. Some—for example, gas meters—measure volume directly. Others measure it indirectly. Orifice and venturi meters, for example, measure it in terms of differential pressure; the rotameter measures it in terms of a variable area; and meters employing rotating elements, induced voltages, magnetic resonance, and heat transfer measure it in terms of velocity and current.

Poor: Assuming that the level of per capita consumption prior to World War II was higher than will be reached currently or in the near future because of normal shifts in the position of rice in the diet as consumer income rises (i.e., a staple as opposed to a specialty packaged food item), increases in sales of rice will follow population growth rather than large increases in per capita consumption in Europe.

Better: It has been suggested that in Europe, rice forms a smaller portion of a person's diet as his standard of living rises. If this is so, the downward trend in total consumption since World War II can be reversed only by population growth, not by greater per capita use.

Poor: For a fuller understanding and appreciation of employee situations as related to career development dead-end levels in an organization of the complexity and at the same time relatively small size of the FCC, there are a number of job classifications which represent what can be described as "dead-end" jobs, since there are few grade levels involved, few positions available and a definite grade ceiling on what represents the top job in these classifications, and they do not represent a long-range career opportunity.

Better: Government employees in agencies such as the FCC have a problem with career development. Because the organization is small and complex, only a few positions are available and the grade levels for these positions are limited. In fact, even the top job in each classification has a restrictive grade ceiling. Consequently, these jobs do not represent long-range career opportunities.

Establish the Proper Relationship Between Ideas

Poor: Vinyl siding seems to have recovered and is now moving along at a healthy growth rate. Seen in perspective, it still accounts for less than 3 percent of the national siding market, compared with aluminum's 28 percent and steel's 1 percent.

Better: Vinyl siding seems to have recovered and is now moving along at a healthy growth rate. Nevertheless, it still accounts for less than 3 percent of the national market for siding, better than steel's 1 percent, but far below aluminum's 28 percent.

Poor: The primary focus on increased profitability from market planning must be on the development of new products and broadened applications of existing products.

Better: If market planning is to contribute to increased profit, its primary focus must be on the development of new products and broader applications of existing products.

Avoid Suggesting That Terms Are Mutually Exclusive When They Are Not

Poor: Of the eight new employees, three are black and two are women.

Better: Of the eight new employees, three are black males, and two are white females.

or

Of the eight new employees, two are black females and one is a black male.

Identify the Source of a Statement

Poor: It is expected that the new product will appeal to consumers of all ages.

Better: An analysis of consumer preferences shows that the new product will appeal to people of all ages.

Poor: It is believed that a work stoppage can be avoided.

Better: According to union and management representatives, a work stoppage can be avoided.

These guidelines merely point up the most common causes of and cures for unclear writing. The fundamental cause of unclear writing is, of course, unclear thinking. We often fail to crystallize our ideas before expressing them. The result is often a memo such as the following:

To: All Instructors

From: Chairman, Division of Evening Studies

Subject: Smoking and Corridor Cleanliness

It has been reported that a survey of the school corridors relative to debris, corridor partition cleanliness, cigarette butts, and burned tiles is in large part due to the Evening School student body. All DES instructors are herewith notified that they are expected to exert a reasonable effort to maintain a satisfactory degree of cleanliness within their area of influence. It was reported that a partition was kicked in during an evening session. Please attempt to keep students from leaning against the corridor walls and marking them with foot and heel prints.

The problem with writing like that is that the writer attempts to refine with a profusion of words a basic idea that does not express what he intended to say. If you analyze the opening sentence of that memo by reducing it to its fundamental elements (subject and predicate), you will find that the sentence says:

It has been reported that ... a survey ... is due to the Evening School student body.

I am sure that the writer intended to convey that the Evening School student body had been littering the corridors and soiling the walls. The use of the word "survey" is interesting. I had the opportunity to ask the author of that memo about his source of information. "Who reported it?" I asked. "Why?" he returned. "Because the source provides credibility," I argued. "If the day students are the source, I wouldn't attach as much credibility to their allegations as I would to the statements of the staff or faculty, for example." "No one reported it," he explained. "I saw it." His use of the word *survey,* therefore, denoted a 'comprehensive view' rather than someone walking around gathering people's opinions. As a graduate of an engineering school, he told me that he was taught never to identify himself by a personal pronoun; therefore, he used the inaccurate phrase, "It has been reported that."

There is a further difficulty with the memo. Because of the three vague terms—*reasonable effort, satisfactory level of cleanliness,* and *within their area of influence*—contained in the second sentence, any instructor could do absolutely nothing and live within the spirit of that memo. Finally, even in the last sentence, the author does not say what he means. "Please attempt to" does not mean "Please see to it that . . ." No writer can expect appropriate action to be taken if he does not stipulate precisely what he wants.

CONCISENESS

Conciseness is closely related to clarity and comprehension. To be concise is not to be brief. If brevity were the goal, to say nothing would be the hallmark of success. To be concise is to express a thought clearly and completely in the fewest words possible. Concise writing makes maximum use of every word. No word is needless.

To express a thought, we need only a subject and a predicate. For example, "Men work" is syntactically complete, but it provides only minimal information. By adding qualifying words and phrases, we can provide more definitive information. Note how each of the following additions contributes to the specificity of the thought:

Men work.

Some men work.

Some men work occasionally.

Some men work occasionally on difficult assignments.

Every word used in the foregoing examples is contributing to the expansion of the idea. Note in the following further expansion, however, that three of the words do not contribute; hence, the sentence is not concise.

Some men work occasionally on difficult assignments in ~~the field of~~ chemistry.

Some people may argue that the addition of the three words in this example does not interfere with the clarity of the sentence. Perhaps not. But verbose writing is undisciplined writing; and to the undisciplined writer, it is an easy step from two or three unnecessary words to a proliferation of unnecessary words, as in the following sentence:

~~For information to be conveyed in an effective manner, an essential requirement is that~~ reports ~~of all types~~ should ~~communicate data in such a way that as to~~ be clear and ~~at the same time~~ concise.

Even if your sentences contain only a few unnecessary words, remember that reports should consider the reader. The cumulative effect of unnecessary words is that the reader must spend a great deal of time extracting information that could be gained in less time. It is a simple matter of arithmetic. A memo or report typed double-spaced on 8½-by-11-inch paper contains between 250 and 350 words, depending on the size of the type face. Let's assume an average of 300 words per page. The average sentence length is from 10 to 15 words. (Count your own average sentence length.) If we assume 10 words per sentence, then the average page contains 30 sentences; if we assume 15 words, the average page contains 20 sentences. Experience shows that a 10-word sentence contains an average of 2 unnecessary words per sentence and that a 15-word sentence contains 4 unnecessary words. On that basis, each page containing 10-word sentences has 60 unnecessary words and each page containing 15-word sentences contains 80 unnecessary words. Therefore, in a 5-page report, the reader is forced to read 300 to 400 unnecessary words; in effect, what is said in five pages could be said in 4 pages or fewer. Thus, the average reader spends about one minute unnecessarily on each five pages. Small wonder that readers complain about the inordinate amount of time required to read reports!

To eliminate unnecessary pages, therefore, we must begin by eliminating unnecessary words. The following guidelines point up the most common sources of verbosity and how they can be eliminated.

Use One Noun Instead of Two (One as an Adjective) Whenever You Can

Poor: In an emergency situation

Better: In an emergency

Poor: The education process is deteriorating.

Better: Education is deteriorating.

Poor: The prestige factor is important.

Better: Prestige is important.

Use the Verb Form Rather Than the Noun Form of a Word Whenever You Can

Poor: The shipment of equipment was made in September and installation took place in October.

Better: The equipment was shipped in September and installed in October.

Poor: The new design should achieve an improvement in the range of the missile.

Better: The new design should improve the range of the missile.

Use a Verb Rather Than a Verbal (a Word Ending in -ing) and a Verb Whenever You Can

Poor: The processing of information is accomplished by the use of machines.

Better: Machines process information.

Poor: Designing the curriculum for the seminar has been undertaken by the Training Department.

Better: The Training Department is designing the curriculum for the seminar.

Replace A Phrase With a Word Whenever You Can

Needless Words: He attended the course on a voluntary basis.

Better: He attended the course voluntarily.

Needless Words: The report contained information of a financial nature.

Better: The report contained financial information.

Replace a Clause With a Word or Phrase When You Can

Needless Words: The container is made of material which is strong and durable.

Better: The container is strong and durable.

Needless Words: Those who are experienced machinists

Better: Experienced machinists

Needless Words: Those who have been granted security clearance

Better: Those with security clearance

Eliminate Awkward Constructions

Awkward: On the basis of improved design, the capacity of the plant has been increased.

Better: Improved design has increased the capacity of the plant.

Awkward: In the case of toxic materials, the company plans to provide improved storage.

Better: The company plans to provide improved storage of toxic materials.

Eliminate Redundant Expressions

Redundant: The personnel department receives approximately 25 to 35 applications for employment each week.

Better: The personnel department receives 25 to 35 applications for employment each week.

Redundant: He is currently visiting the West Coast.

Better: He is visiting the West Coast.

Redundant: When documents are photocopied, red is a color that appears as black.

Better: When documents are photocopied, red appears black.

Redundant: The Gross National Product should continue to increase in the future.

Better: The Gross National Product should continue to increase.

Redundant: The company paid its highest dividend in the year 1976.

Better: The company paid its highest dividend in 1976.

Redundant: At this point in time we have not decided whether to increase our prices.

Better: We have not decided whether to increase our prices.

Eliminate Unnecessary Verb Forms

Unnecessary Words: The cost estimate submitted includes any maintenance involved.

Better: The cost estimate includes maintenance.

Unnecessary Words: The training program provided consists of lectures and problem solving.

Better: The training program consists of lectures and problem solving.

Eliminate Indirect Constructions

Weak and Wordy: It is the purpose of this report to discuss three new-product opportunities.

Better: This report discusses three new-product opportunities.

Weak and Wordy: It is management's contention that the union's demands are exorbitant.

Better: Management believes that the union's demands are exorbitant.

Weak and Wordy: There are occasions when building materials are in short supply.

Better: Building materials are occasionally in short supply.

Weak and Wordy: There is a new development in computer technology which will revolutionize the industry.

Better: A new development in computer technology will revolutionize the industry.

Combine Simple Ideas

Wordy: There are four ABC sales offices. All are located on the East Coast.

Better: All four ABC sales offices are located on the East Coast.

Wordy: J.D. Powers is 38 years old. He has been president of the company for seven years.

Better: At 38 years old, J.D. Powers has been president of the company for seven years.

Conciseness, of course, applies to more than just the syntax of sentences. In larger perspective, it involves irrelevant material, which abounds in all sorts of documents. Letters, for example, frequently contain needless paragraphs perhaps because the writer feels that if he restricts himself only to the information that is needed, the words will seem sparse in comparison with the size of the sheet on which they appear. Consequently, stereotypic paragraphs are inserted as introductions and conclusions only because the writer is concerned more with an aesthetic sense of balance than with information that is pertinent. Similarly, in proposals, information well known to the reader is included as a section devoted to background, consisting frequently of a history of the organization or of a recounting of its products, processes, or policies. In much the same way, formal reports often include all the information the writer collected, without considering whether it is necessary or even relevant. As a result, reports often raise more questions than they answer.

The aim of conciseness, then, is not merely to economize on words, but to enhance ideas.

STYLE

Very few people look forward to reading reports and memos. Even when the subject matter is important or appealing, readers frequently skim through the contents to extract only the salient ideas. Why? Usually because the writing is dull even if not difficult. Often cluttered by awkward constructions, artificial conventions, endless qualifications, and unintelligible jargon, the prose hobbles along instead of marching.

The arthritic condition of most business and technical writing is largely the result of misguided notions that style is mere ornament superimposed on substance, and that there is a universal style that should be applied to reports. The extension of this kind of thinking leads to the belief that as long as this "technical" or "business" style is slavishly followed, effective communication will develop as naturally as second teeth. This assumption, of course, is as ridiculous as contending that every baseball player will automatically hit home runs if he uses Hank Aaron's bat.

Style is as personal as a signature. A product of such factors as education, environment, personality, and perception, it combines spontaneity and discipline. In so doing, it allows each writer to create a natural, fluent, and forceful prose by selecting from a variety of linguistic options the ones most appropriate to his purpose, his audience, and his subject.

Each option is simply a means of achieving a desired rhetorical objective: emphasis, vigor, variety, rhythm, tone, pace. Although an effective style cannot be developed mechanically, it requires a knowledge of the mechanics of composition. Here are some guidelines for developing your personal style.

Emphasis

Don't Give Two Thoughts Equal Weight When One is More Important Than the Other

Poor: I was cashing a check and five armed men held up the bank.

Improved: While I was cashing a check, five armed men held up the bank.

Poor: A generator at Niagara Falls failed, and the East Coast was blacked out.

Improved: The East Coast was blacked out because a generator at Niagara Falls failed.

Don't Emphasize the Less Important of Two Thoughts (Upside-Down Subordination)

Poor: Although the chief reason for the decline in profit was a 40 percent drop in sales, increased production costs also contributed to the problem.

Improved: Although increased production costs contributed to the problem, the chief reason for the decline in profit was a 40 percent drop in sales.

Poor: There was a malfunction in the computer, causing billings of over $2 million to be delayed.

Improved: Billings of over $2 million were delayed because of a computer malfunction.

When Expressing Two or More Elements in a Series, Make the Construction Parallel

Weak: About half the residents were asked to stop taking showers and water their lawns while crews repaired the broken water main.

Improved: About half the residents were asked not to take showers or water their lawns while crews repaired the broken water main.

Weak: The financial statement was incomplete, unclear, and contained inaccuracies.

Improved: The financial statement was incomplete, unclear, and inaccurate.

Weak: The product is convenient, simply designed, and it doesn't cost much.

Improved: The product is convenient, simply designed, and inexpensive.

For Greater Emphasis, Invert the Natural Word Order

Natural Order: The tired and hungry technicians worked until all equipment was operating.

Inverted Order: The technicians, tired and hungry, worked until all equipment was operating.

Natural Order: The writer who can prepare an effective report effortlessly is rare indeed.

Inverted Order: Rare indeed is the writer who can prepare an effective report effortlessly.

Natural Order: The auditor checked the records carefully and patiently.

Inverted Order: Carefully and patiently, the auditor checked the records.

Natural Order: The report provides extensive data for those interested in detailed analysis.

Inverted Order: For those interested in detailed analysis, the report provides extensive data.

Position Words and Phrases as Close as Possible to the Ideas They are Intended to Emphasize

Weak: He primarily works on management problems.

Better: He works primarily on management problems.

Weak: He only requested a small budget for the project.

Better: He requested only a small budget for the project.

Weak: The morale of the department was improved by an adjustment of salaries, as well as productivity.

Better: The morale of the department, as well as its productivity, was improved by an adjustment of salaries.

or

Not only morale but also productivity was increased by an adjustment of salaries.

Vigor

Prefer the Active to the Passive Voice

Weak: A study to determine the efficiency of the new system was undertaken by the committee.

Improved: The committee studied the new system to determine its efficiency.

Weak: The recommendation was made by the school committee that four schools be closed.

Improved: The school committee recommended that four schools be closed.

Weak: It has been shown by experience that more money than has been allocated by management is usually required for new plant construction.

Improved: Experience shows that construction of a new plant usually requires more money than management allocates.

Use the Passive Voice When:

1. *The Agent Is Unknown—*

   The third shift was cancelled because of inclement weather.

   He was hurt in an automobile accident.

   At least 40 names were added to the list of contributors.

2. *The Receiver Is More Important Than the Agent—*

   John P. Sherwood was elected to the city council.

   A check for $100,000 was presented to the school by a representative of Piedmont Plastics Co.

3. *A Weak Substitute for the Imperative is Appropriate—*

   Reports should be prepared carefully.

   Expense accounts should be approved by the appropriate department manager.

Avoid Excessive Predication

Weak: The tendency of the average motorist is to wait until the first snowfall before putting on snow tires.

Improved: The average motorist waits until the first snowfall before he puts on his snow tires.

Weak: The reason for the company's use of automatic equipment in preference to manually operated equipment is to take advantage of its faster report collating capability.

Improved: The company uses automatic equipment because it collates reports faster than manually operated equipment.

Weak: The results of the study are in good agreement with those of earlier studies.

Improved: The results of this study agree with those of earlier studies.

or

The results of this study corroborate those of earlier studies.

Weak: The theory is that greater machine utilization will result in lower personnel costs.

Improved: Theoretically, as more machines are used, the cost of labor decreases.

or

Theoretically, the greater the number of machines, the lower the cost of labor.

Weak: A sufficiently large inventory of spare parts exists in the company.

Improved: The company has an adequate supply of spare parts.

Variety

The dullness of technical and business reports can be traced largely to the monotony of the sentences. They are much like an endless parade of soldiers dressed in fatigues, in which individual identity is lost and the constant repetition creates tedium.

Parades hold our interest because they blend different types of units in different uniforms. We are less conscious of length in the midst of variety. So, too, with reports. By varying the syntactical pattern of sentences, you can make the discussion move easily so that the reader becomes less conscious of volume.

To provide variety, you can use sentences of different lengths and of different syntactical arrangements. Varying the length depends on the number of ideas you wish to convey, the relationships you wish to establish, and the amount of modifiers you consider necessary. Varying the syntactical arrangement, in general, depends on whether you wish to express the main idea at the beginning or at the end, or to balance two equally important ideas.

If you want to express the main idea at the beginning, you can select from among the following syntactical variations:

Nouns

Efficiency and productivity go hand in hand.

Workers in industry today receive far higher wages and fringe benefits than their ancestors because of the influence of unions and the competition for skilled labor.

Adjectives

Careful and extensive evaluation of performance criteria requires patience and understanding.

An engaging style helps a writer to convey his message, especially when the subject matter is difficult or unappealing.

Adverbs

Carefully and methodically, the personnel manager screened the applications.

Essentially, each section of the report is a discussion of each criterion used in the evaluation of the system.

Prepositional Phrases

During the interview the candidate appeared to be nervous, perhaps because he did not know what to expect.

For three hours service was interrupted while an electrician repaired the lines.

Correlatives

Neither labor nor management objected to the contract.

Not only quality but also cost was considered in the selection of the furniture for the conference room.

Noun Clauses

Whoever is given responsibility should also be given authority.

What one employee considers acceptable another may not.

Gerunds

Increasing the department's productivity is the principal goal for the coming year.

Operating a multicolor press requires more skill than operating a one-color press.

If you want to suspend the main idea until the end of the sentence, you can choose from among these constructions as well as from some of the ones listed above:

Participial Phrase

Having developed and tested the new product, the company is interested in beginning limited production.

Convinced that the marketing plan had merit, the company adopted it in 1976.

Infinitive Phrase

To diversify its product line and acquire greater working capital, Hilo Products merged with Broadwell Plastics.

To ensure job satisfaction and better performance, management establishes goals with the assistance of employees.

Adverbial Clause

Because the weather in the Northeast was less severe than expected and many former consumers of oil changed to other forms of energy, there was no shortage of oil for home heating during the winter.

So that more employees can form car pools, lists of home addresses have been distributed.

Appositive

A recognized expert in nuclear engineering, George Babson is frequently consulted about the construction of reactors.

Nominative Absolute

Cost being the sole consideration, many sophisticated systems were rejected.

A third way of varying the syntactical pattern of a sentence is to use a balanced construction. This technique is frequently used to enhance a comparison or contrast. Note the difference in the following sentences.

Not Balanced: Authority is commensurate with responsibility.

Balanced: The greater the authority, the greater the responsibility.

Not Balanced: Those who are guilty of racial prejudice deny people their fundamental rights.

Balanced: To harbor racial prejudice is to deny human rights.

Not Balanced: The company's strength lies in its marketing; its service, however, is weak.

Balanced: The company is strong in marketing, but weak in service.

Pace

Pace is the rate at which the writer communicates information. It should be governed by the reader's familiarity with the subject and the complexity of the concept or topic being discussed. Since familiarity and complexity may vary from topic to topic, the pace should be varied accordingly. For example, if you are merely reviewing a known principle, a procedure, or a situation as a prelude to a discussion of less familiar aspects, the pace can be quickened. When the more complex issues are discussed, the pace can be slowed. In general, pace is governed by the mass and proportion of detail included in a discussion. The greater the detail, the slower the pace.

To quicken the pace:

Keep your sentence constructions simple.

Use the active voice.

Use parallel constructions.

Tabulate items in a series.

To slow the pace:

Increase the number of ideas in sentences.

Increase the modification.

Use purposeful repetition, such as paraphrases.

Use examples and analogies.

Use the passive voice.

Introduce deliberate pauses by changing the normal word order or by setting ideas between dashes.

Introduce tables and graphs.

Rhythm

Rhythm is a matter of word order. Each word has certain accented and unaccented syllables. For example:

design   diligently   priority

Thus, as we read words in combination, the regularity of the interval between stresses creates the rhythm of the sentence. Consider these sentences.

1. To be easy to read, a report should be clear and concise.

2. The warehouse space-use study took four months to complete.

The first sentence is easier to read than the second sentence even though they both contain approximately the same number of words and a simple idea. The first sentence flows easily because the interval between stresses is fairly regular. In the second sentence, the arrangement of words creates an irregular cadence—that is, three stresses in succession—and thus creates a jarring effect. With stress marks included, we can see the difference in rhythm:

1. Tŏ bĕ éaśy tŏ réad, ă rĕpórt shŏuld bĕ cleár aňd cŏnciśe.

2. Thĕ wárehŏuse spáce-uśe śtudў toók foúr moňths tŏ cŏmpléte.

Note the difference in rhythm when the second thought is expressed in a slightly different construction:

Hŏw wárehŏuse spáce ĭs uśed rĕquíred foúr moňths ŏf stúdў.

In discussing clarity, we said to position modifiers as close as possible to the terms they modify. To write prose that moves easily, however, you must also be aware that a modifier's position may satisfy the demands of syntax but create an unnatural rhythm.

Poor: The editor revised extensively the report.

Better: The editor revised the report extensively.

Similarly, in a sentence containing a series, the position of the term containing the most modification affects the rhythm.

Poor: The company manufactures a uniquely designed refrigeration unit, stoves, and washers.

Better: The company manufactures stoves, washers, and a uniquely designed refrigeration unit.

Rhythm and structure are inseparable; therefore, it is important to be conscious of the sound of your prose as well as the sense, for rhythm contributes to the rate at which information is assimilated.

TONE

All writing is an attempt to influence the reader to accept the writer's explanations, convictions, or suggestions. The writer's words, therefore, must project reasonableness, sincerity, confidence, consideration, and objectivity. These qualities are conveyed by the tone of the writing.

Tone is affected by failure to consider the audience's background. If, for example, a knowledgeable audience is given unnecessary detail about a subject, the tone conveys condescension. Similarly, if the writer fails to supply enough detail to an audience unfamiliar with a subject, he will be accused of being inconsiderate or perhaps even arrogant.

Some writers create an impression of uncertainty by overqualifying their statements of fact. Such statements as "It is estimated that approximately 10 to 20 programming errors are introduced through carelessness" debilitates the effect of the intended evidence. Other writers inadvertently lessen assurance by introducing unnecessary words or phrases. For example, to write "This report is an attempt to evaluate the performance of the department" suggests that the writer is not certain that he has fulfilled the objective. By writing "This report evaluates the performance of the department," he eliminates doubt.

Undue apology and feeble attempts to justify a policy or procedure also convey a lack of confidence. Consider, for example, this memo.

Although this may at first seem a near unpalatable communication, I feel there is reasonable justification on my part for initiating the following request.

I feel it is only responsible on my part to tighten up on the ever-increasing number of irresponsible and isolated statements made to the media, more often than not without my knowledge and consequently without my support or approval. Such statements suggest that we lack a cohesive policy and a common objective.

To eliminate these fractured attempts at statements of policy, please consider the following points effective immediately:

1. Each division manager is responsible for reviewing all statements submitted to the media.

2. Such statements must be prepared in writing for my approval before any release is made.

I apologize to you again for what I know must strike you as an unduly harsh action. But I can only justify it again by making clear to you that it is the only way we can reduce the inexcusable number of misstatements of policy being disseminated publicly.

The tone of the foregoing memo creates additional difficulty, in that within the context of apology are subjective evaluations indiscreetly stated in such words as "irresponsible" and "inexcusable." As a result, their irritating effect is enhanced.

Similarly, a negative tone often heightens irritation or disappointment by stressing what cannot or will not be done. By contrast, a positive tone plays down limitations by emphasizing what can or will be done.

Negative: Those traveling on company business will not be reimbursed for first-class fare.

Positive: Those traveling on company business will be reimbursed only for the lowest available fare, which is normally tourist class.

Negative: We cannot complete the study until June 30.

Positive: We will complete the study by June 30.

The style so prevalent in business and technical reports is an artifact of those who are tone deaf. Labored and impersonal, it is concerned more with writing words to dignify the writer than with communicating ideas to help the reader. Consider, for example, this advice, written in a style that Jacques Barzun has called "modern Micawber."

> In the current circumstances in which extreme optimism characterizes the prices being paid for ownership or ownership interests in American business, it is our considered opinion that one of the primary tasks of the investor is to attempt to minimize exposure to erosion of capital against the time when such optimism evaporates and is succeeded by a thoughtful, sober, realistic general approach to value and earning power.

By contrast, consider the same idea expressed in a tone that suggests that reader and writer are on the same level.

> Prices being paid today for ownership or control of a business are inflated because buyers are unduly optimistic about the future. To conserve our capital, we should wait until the stock market reflects a more realistic view of the value and earning power of the dollar.

The first version suggests pronouncement; the second, conviction. The tone of the first suggests that superior wisdom is being carefully measured out by someone unaffected by the problem. The tone of the second suggests a candid opinion about how to solve a common problem.

Finally, if you have to write a memo in which you cannot comply or can only partially comply with a request, the tone of your response is important. Consider, for example, the two versions below. The original version would probably nettle the recipient because it sounds arbitrary, autocratic, and intransigent. The second suggests a desire to cooperate and arrive at a reasonable solution.

Original	Revised
I have recently ordered forty 5-drawer filing cabinets for staff use. Unfortunately, 73 people throughout the company have requested filing cabinets. I believe that one 5-drawer cabinet per person per department is enough. According to an inventory made last month, your department has one cabinet per person.	At present, the number of requests for file cabinets is about double the number of cabinets available. While we want to make every effort to satisfy staff requirements, we also want to make certain that existing file space is being used effectively.
Therefore, your department will not receive any additional file cabinets at this time. I request your cooperation in emptying some cabinets by shipping old material to the central storage area and sharing cabinets with your staff who have requested cabinets.	We suggest as a guideline that you evaluate your needs on the basis of one 5-drawer cabinet per person in your department. This guideline is suggested in recognition of the fact that most files contain three categories of material: (1) that which is used regularly, (2) that which is used occasionally, and (3) that which is used rarely.
	If you will review your files and cull the material used rarely, we will arrange to store it for you in the central storage area and make it available to you whenever you need it. You may also find that the material used only occasionally can be filed in a shared cabinet.

> If after completing this
> reevaluation, you still require
> additional file cabinets, please
> resubmit your needs. We hope, in
> this way, to be able to fill them on
> an equitable basis.
>
> Thank you for your
> cooperation.

Remember, then, that your credibility and effectiveness are affected by the reader's perception of you. And perception is often influenced more by *how* you say something than by *what* you say. It is a matter of tone.

EXERCISES

1. Make the following ideas clear.
    a. He is doing extensive research on the nuclear genetics of invertebrates, like me.
    b. Since his appointment as corporate counsel, Mr. Smith has been responsible for all of the company's legal problems.
    c. Three classes of data were obtained: male income, female income, commuting distances, commuting times, and average hours worked.
    d. His assignment was evaluating the effect of relocating the international airport on residents of the surrounding area.
    e. In one day we crossed a region which our grandparents took two months to cross in an airplane.
    f. In 1978, 89 banks submitted their data for participation in the Functional Cost Program. This compares to a similar 89 banks for the previous year. However, the number of member banks declined so that participation actually denotes a slight gain from the previous year.
    g. I hope that you received the road information necessary for your emergency trip from the state police.
    h. I was backing my car out of the driveway in the usual manner, when it was struck by the other car in the same place it had been struck several times before.

     i. Unique formats shall not be used in government reports unless specifically approved for use by your company.

     j. The new employee became angry when a colleague tried to offer advice, which was neither tactful nor appropriate.

2. Make the following sentences concise.

     a. The manpower forecast is a method for analyzing past and projecting future manpower utilization patterns in order to determine future manpower requirements.

     b. Development of an energy resource base can only be efficiently accomplished if the company is aware of the technological and scientific state of affairs.

     c. The proposed new airport will create a situation in which noise will be a problem.

     d. In the case of experiments with mice, it was proved that smoking causes forms of cancer.

     e. In terms of checking accounts, it is interesting to note that there is a significantly larger number maintained in banks that do not require a minimum balance.

     f. The estimated margin for the department in 1979 was approximately 10 percent of sales.

     g. In today's volatile economic and social environment, it is essential that the planning and decision-making process for a college be structured so that the governing body can be presented complete and comprehensive data.

     h. During the course of the study, interviews were conducted with leading citizens by the research team in order to obtain information relevant to the desirability of constructing the new post office in close proximity to the Pine Bluffs shopping center.

     i. We wish to announce the annual meeting of the Credit Union, which will be held in the auditorium on January 27 at 10 A.M.

     j. A need for a broader product line exists within the company.

     k. There are three operating divisions in the company. They occupy separate buildings.

     l. The average annual salary of secretaries in this area is $12,000 per year.

m. There were at least 100 names that we added to the list.

n. The elimination of postmarking mail in each intermediate post office was made a number of years ago in order to effect reductions in cost and to speed up mail delivery.

o. He effected a change in the department's organizational structure.

3. Rewrite the following paragraph to eliminate the monotonous primer style.

> An audience needs three pieces of information. These are necessary to give the audience perspective about your speech. The audience first needs to know what the talk is about. It needs to know this in terms of the central theme not just a general topic. The audience also needs some background information. The amount you must provide depends on your audience. It depends on how familiar they are with the reason for your talk. The audience also needs to be told the major areas you intend to discuss in support of your central theme. These areas should be described in your opening remarks. These three pieces of information will make your audience better prepared. They will help them to assimilate and understand the details presented in the body of your speech.

4. Rewrite the following memo.

To: Entire Staff

From: Telephone Supervisor

Subject: Telephone Service

This memo is in response to a series of recent staff complaints about telephone service, service at the switchboard, and lost calls that were beyond the control of the Company operator, in the telephone network trunks.

The Company target date to have a new telephone system on line is 8 to 12 months. In the interim, there are plans to expand our present system and add staff at the switchboard as needed to keep up with staff requirements for these services. At present our Chief Operator is training operators who were hired as staff additions. With this additional help, the operators should be able to answer promptly as they had before. These modifications are routine assignments for the Telecommunications Department.

Our telephone system gets heavy use. For example, on a typical day staff telephones are picked up 16,000 times to make an internal call, dial 9, reach the operator, etc., and 4300 calls come into the Company. We now have a total of 160 lines leased from the Telephone Company to keep in working order. Because of heavy usage and the age of our system there are resulting repair problems ranging from lights out on a telephone to call cut-offs. The former is usually easily remedied; the latter problem may be caused by malfunctioning equipment at our switchboard, Telephone Company equipment in their massive telephone network at the distant end, and on occasion human error. To get at the source of the problem, we need information when your problem happens and as specific data as possible. When you call 500, the Chief Operator logs in the problem and refers it to the appropriate Telephone Company personnel for action. She will follow up on the problem until we have a resolution. The Company has experienced periodic, unscheduled service interruptions in this year, which the Telephone Company says are due to the construction project at Tulip Plaza, interference with the cables which supply service to our trunk lines. We will alert the Telephone Company as often as required as it is their responsibility to maintain our system.

I repeat, please call 500 or 501 to report any unusual telephone conditions which you encounter and as soon as they occur. Your response and cooperation will assist in a more timely resolution of repair problems as well as highlight any major deficiencies in our internal system.

7
Using Tables and Illustrations

NEED FOR DISPLAYING INFORMATION

Words are sometimes inadequate to convey a message completely, accurately, and clearly. They must be supplemented by a picture, a diagram, a sketch, a graph, or a table. These kinds of aids help the reader to understand relationships, follow instructions, make comparisons, and identify trends more quickly and conveniently than a word description. Consider, for example, this textual discussion of statistics.

> Trichlorethylene consumption rose from 422 million pounds in 1960 to about 530 million pounds in 1965. The major end use—metal degreasing—grew 75 million pounds, from 360 million pounds in 1960 to 435 million pounds in 1965. This use accounted for 85 percent of total trichlorethylene consumption in 1960, but for only 82 percent in 1965. The second-largest end use—as a precursor to perchlorethylene—remained essentially unchanged at 50 million pounds during the same period, although it rose to 80 million pounds during the first two years of the period. Nevertheless, because of the overall increase in trichlorethylene consumption, this end use accounted for 11 percent in 1960 but for 9 percent in 1965. Solvent extraction likewise remained unchanged at 7 million pounds during the period, but its percentage of total consumption declined slightly, from 2 percent in 1960 to slightly over 1 percent in 1965. The major increase occurred in the miscellaneous category, which grew from 5 million pounds in 1960 to 38 million pounds in 1965, primarily because of increased use of trichlorethylene paint for metal-product finishing.

Did you grasp all of the detail? Did you find it difficult to compare all of the pieces of information? Numerical information interspersed throughout text is very difficult to retain.

Presenting the information in tabular form allows the reader to digest it at a more leisurely pace and to establish relationships more easily and comprehensively. It also allows the writer to support the main point he wishes to convey by providing a convenient reference. The reader can thus concentrate on the commentary without the need to remember the statistical detail. Thus, the same information can be conveyed much more effectively like this:

Trichlorethylene consumption increased over 100 million pounds from 1960 to 1965. (See Table 1.) Although metal degreasing—the principal end use—accounted for the largest absolute increase, miscellaneous uses represent the largest percentage increase, primarily because of the increased use of trichlorethylene in paint for metal-product finishing.

Table 1 TRICHLORETHYLENE CONSUMPTION 1960-1965

End Use	1960		1965	
	Millions of Pounds	%	Millions of Pounds	%
Metal Degreasing	360	85	435	82.0
Precursor to Perchlorethylene	50	12	50	9.4
Solvent Extraction	7	2	7	1.3
Miscellaneous	5	1	38	7.3
TOTAL	422	100	530	100

Similarly, visualizing something—especially something unfamiliar—solely by a verbal description is very difficult. Consider, for example, this description.

The configuration consists of five rectangles, labeled A, B, C, D, and E from top to bottom, respectively. Each is approximately 3/8-inch wide and 3/4-inch long. Rectangle A is at a 45-degree angle to B in such a way that with the long dimension viewed as the base, the lower left-hand corner of A touches the upper left-hand corner of B, with B positioned so that its short side is the base. Rectangle B is at a 90-degree angle to the left of C; that is, the long dimension of B is vertical and touching the short dimension of C so that the short dimension of B is a continuation of the long dimension of C. Rectangle D is parallel to A in such a way that the midpoint of the upper long side of D touches the lower right-hand corner of C. Rectangle E is parallel with and touching D so that the right-hand short dimension of E bisects the lower long dimension of D.

Can you picture the configuration readily? The difficulty is that the writer often must depend on abstract ideas to convey concrete relationships. Therefore, a graphical illustration (as in Figure 3) greatly simplifies something that appears tremendously complex in a written description.

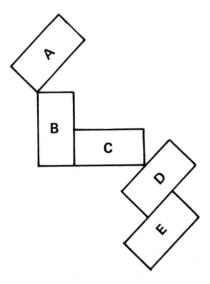

Figure 3   Configuration of Rectangles

APPROPRIATENESS OF EACH FORM

Tabular and graphical displays serve the same purpose as words: they develop and support topic ideas. Sometimes they supplement words, and sometimes they replace them. At all times, however, they should be a clear and concise means of expanding on an idea. Therefore, decide what you want to convey before selecting how you want to convey it.

Showing What Something Looks Like

If you want to show what a concrete object looks like, considerations such as color, size, shape, and arrangement of parts may be important. Consequently, a photograph or a sketch is appropriate. The stage of development, of course, is an additional consideration. If the object is in the conceptual stage, you may be restricted to a sketch. If it is in the production stage, you may feel that a photograph will provide more effective detail.

If you want to show something abstract—such as how a company or division is structured—an organization chart (as in Figure 4) can be used effectively to show the reporting relationships.

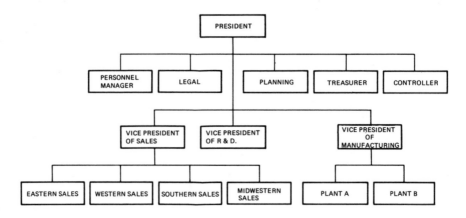

Figure 4   Organization Chart

Occasionally you may want to point up an abstract idea with concrete detail; for example, how people delay the preparation of a report and the resultant crisis that borders on chaos. In such instances, a cartoon may be appropriate (see Figure 5).

Showing How Something Works

If your objective is to show how something works, appearance is secondary to function. Consequently, details such as shape and size may be irrelevant or even obstructive. Therefore, a sketch or schematic is usually appropriate. Although it may be possible in some instances to photograph operating mechanisms, on many occasions the equipment may be too large to photograph in detail (see Figure 6) or the casing or supports may obstruct the operating components. Moreover, even if a photograph gives an unobstructed view, a sketch can provide the additional detail needed to help explain the principle of operation (see Figure 7).

Because graphical illustrations are static and the operation of equipment is dynamic, illustrations are rarely self-explanatory. They are merely convenient references so that the reader can follow the verbal explanation.

Figure 5   Typical Approach to Report Preparation

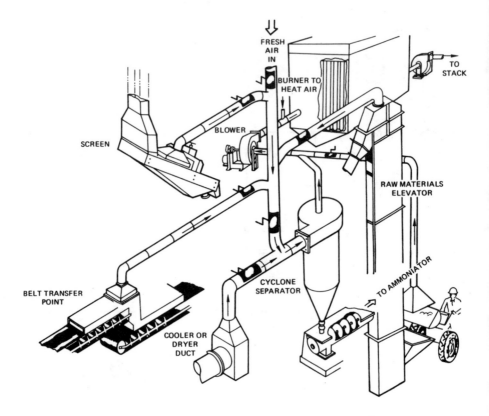

Figure 6 Dust-Collection System

Outlining a Procedure

If you are outlining a simple procedure that progresses in uninterrupted steps, you may need nothing more than an outline of the steps in chronological sequence:

1. Collect Data

2. Analyze Data

3. Organize the Report

4. Prepare the First Draft

5. Evaluate and Edit

If, however, the procedure is more complex—for example, if operations are occurring simultaneously and if the sequence is interrupted at various points—a flow chart is more appropriate. Suppose, for example, that you wanted to identify the phases and steps involved in

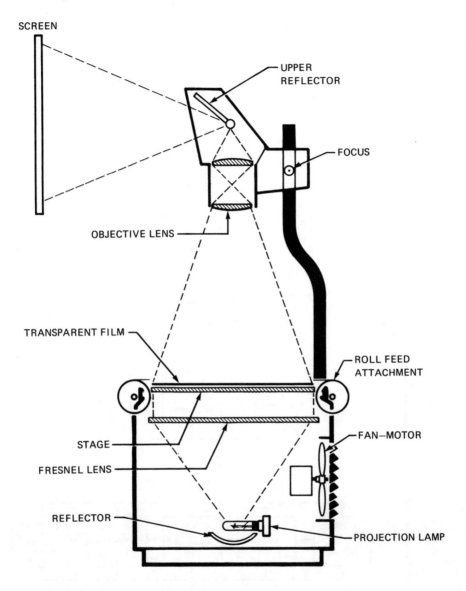

Figure 7   Overhead Projector

establishing an oil or gas field. You might choose to portray it like the flow chart in Figure 8.

As in the explanation of the operation of equipment, each step is the subject of additional discussion. The diagram helps to provide cohesion and perspective.

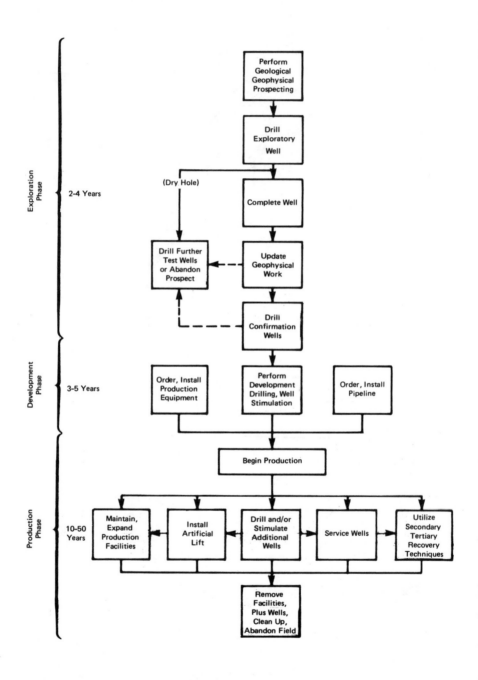

Figure 8   Steps in Establishing a Producing Oil or Gas Field

Showing the Location of Something

Maps of various types are frequently used in providing directions and in identifying specific locations. In such instances, the maps consist of sketches that identify a specific building in a complex or that show how to reach a specific company, for example, by car or public transportation. In other instances, maps of larger areas are used to show such things as the locations of regional offices, population concentrations, agricultural and industrial activities, and consumer preferences.

Like other graphical illustrations, a map is sometimes an alternative to a table when a broad comparison or a perspective is the objective. Consider the map in Figure 9, for example.

The attitudes depicted on the map represent a sampling of 100 locations throughout the 48 contiguous states. If the names of the utility companies and the specific locations were important considerations, a table dividing the states into regions and identifying each

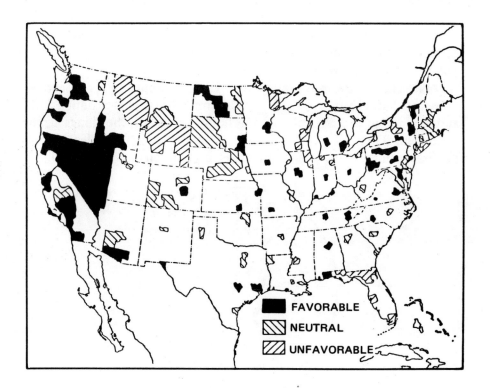

Figure 9   Utility Attitudes Toward Solar Energy Development

company, each location, and each attitude would be a more appropriate display.

Showing Quantitative Relationships

Although flow charts, maps, diagrams, and the like show relationships, they do not always—or even frequently—involve comparisons. Most of the comparisons in business reports involve statistics. Therefore, pie charts, bar graphs, curves, and tables can be used to advantage. In general, graphs are used for making broad comparisons or for identifying trends, because they portray quantitative relationships more clearly and simply than numbers alone. The reader can see, for example, how large something is, how much larger or smaller it is than something else, and how fast it is progressing. When greater detail and precision are needed, however, tables are more appropriate.

A pie chart is used for showing proportions of discontinuous data. A classic example is how the federal budget is allocated in a given fiscal year. Pie charts can also be used to show sales distributions, market shares, product mixes, and relative size of investments in a given area or at a given time. So, for example, if we wanted to show the proportion of a publishing company's textbook sales by geographic area, we might portray it like the pie chart in Figure 10.

Pie charts are not very effective in comparing proportions, however, because they diffuse the differences across two dimensions and compound the difficulty by physically separating the things being compared. Thus, if we use pie charts to compare the sales of two publishers in the same geographic areas, each pie chart is easy to follow,

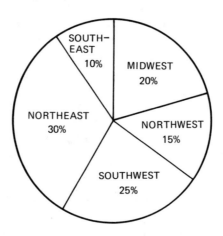

Figure 10 Company A's Sales by Geographic Area

but the percentage differences between the two are less easy to visualize than on a bar graph. In the comparison on the pie charts, the reader depends more on the percentages listed in each segment than on the relative sizes of the segments, whereas the side-by-side comparisons on the bar graph make the differences more evident (see Figures 11 and 12).

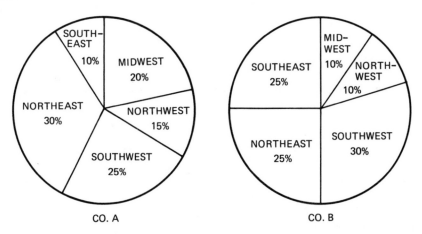

Figure 11 Comparison of Sales by Geographic Area

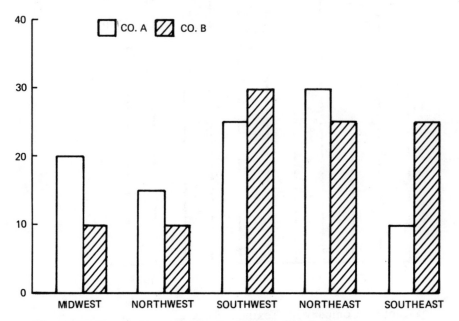

Figure 12 Comparison of Sales by Geographic Area

The segmented bar chart is useful for comparing proportions of one thing over different periods or proportions of two or more things over the same period when the number of proportions (segments) and the relative differences are not great. Suppose, for example, that we wanted to show the percentage of textbook sales accounted for at specific levels of education from 1971 to 1975. Given the differences and number of comparisons, the segmented chart in Figure 13 portrays the variations fairly easily. Note, however, that the precise percentage differences are not as immediately discernible as the visual evidence of increases and decreases. Again, the selection of the display depends on the objective.

If we wished to portray a large number of components fluctuating

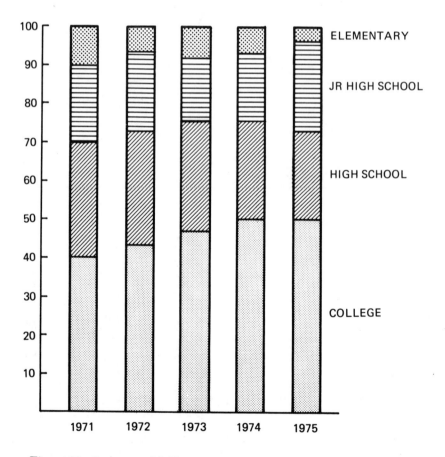

Figure 13 Company A's Textbook Sales

widely over a number of years, the segmented bar chart would lose its effectiveness (see Figure 14).

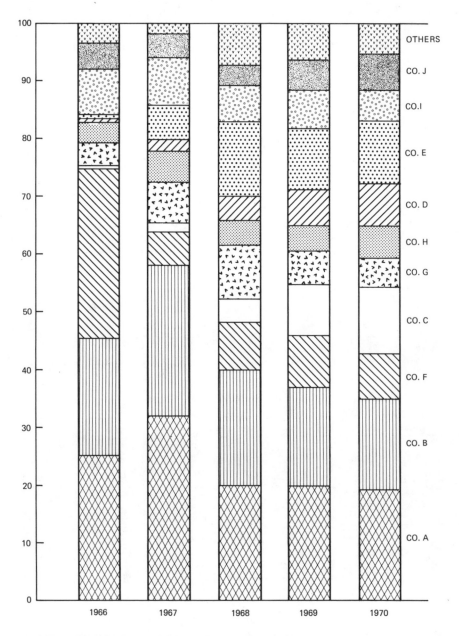

Figure 14   Elementary Textbook Market Shares

In this case, a table would be more appropriate. The construction of the table would depend, of course, on the principal point we wanted to make. For example, if we wanted to show the relative standings in 1970 and how each company had fared in earlier years, we would construct the table like Table 2.

If, however, we wanted to show the position of each company in each year, Table 3 should be used.

Table 2 Elementary Textbook Market Shares

	1966	1967	1968	1969	1970
Co. A	26	32	20	20	19
Co. B	18	26	20	17	16
Co. C	—	1	4	9	10
Co. D	2	4	5	6	9
Co. E	—	7	12	11	9
Co. F	31	6	9	8	8
Co. G	5	4	4	5	7
Co. H	3	7	9	7	6
Co. I	8	9	8	6	6
Co. J	3	2	2	4	4
Others	4	1	7	7	6

Table 3 Elementary Textbook Market Positions

1966	1967	1968	1969	1970
F	A	A	A	A
A	B	B	B	B
B	I	E	E	C
I	E	F	C	D
G	H	H	F	E
H	F	I	H	F
J	D	D	D	G
D	G	C	I	H
C	J	G	G	I
E	C	J	J	J

The following examples show a comparison of three companies over three time periods. Although Figure 15 makes the horizontal differences for each company easy to visualize, it does not provide easy visual comparison vertically.

In such instances, stacked bar graphs, such as Figure 16, are more appropriate.

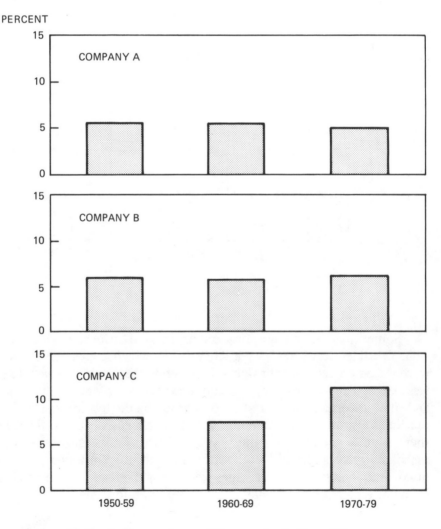

Figure 15 Profit Comparisons of Companies A, B, and C

PERCENT

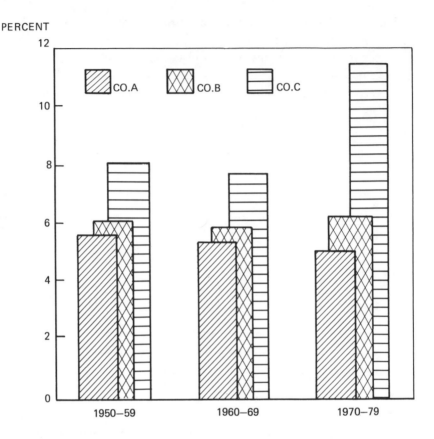

Figure 16   Profit Comparisons of Companies A, B, and C

Sometimes either a table or a graph will point up an analysis equally well. Consider, for example, a situation in which copying machines were placed on each of four floors. To operate the machines, each user was assigned an auditron key that could be used on any of the machines and that recorded the number of copies made by the user. The machines also recorded the number of copies made on them. Because there were fewer users on the first and fourth floors, slightly slower machines were located there. After six months, however, it was discovered that the faster machines were being overused and in need of frequent repair. The following analysis was therefore made.

A comparison of key counts and machine counts indicates that users on floors on which the slower machines are located are making copies elsewhere. The variances suggest that people on the first floor are using the machine on the second floor, and that people on the fourth floor are using the machine on the third floor. Because the capacities of the faster machines are being overextended, breakdowns have become frequent. (See Table 4.)

Table 4 Average Monthly Totals

Location	Machine Count	Key Count by Floor of Users	Key Variance
First Floor	16,960	26,050	+ 9,090
Second Floor	37,500	27,760	- 9,740
Third Floor	41,100	26,450	- 14,650
Fourth Floor	8,530	23,830	+15,300
TOTALS	104,090	104,090	—

Had the analyst elected to show the same results in graphical form, he could have used a bar graph, such as in Figure 17 (see page 122).

The table, of course, points up variances with greater accuracy than the graph. Nevertheless, the graph emphasizes the same point. If the analysis were part of a brief report, the analyst, for the sake of expediency, might choose to use the tabular material since he probably developed the data in this form and it portrays the situation concisely. In an analysis incorporating more extensive and complex data, he might elect to use a graph as a simplified extraction to make his point and might also include the more comprehensive and complex data as an appendix for those who wish to study the details.

Still another graph form—the line graph—is useful in displaying continuous data; that is, the line graph is designed to show change over a given period. Information can be plotted, for example, day by day, week by week, month by month, or year by year. Representing points that are essentially the peaks of a series of bar graphs, line graphs show fluctuations from point to point. Although single line graphs are used in business reports, multiple line graphs comparing things over the same period are more common. Because they are continuous, they are often more effective in enhancing disparities, as in Figure 18.

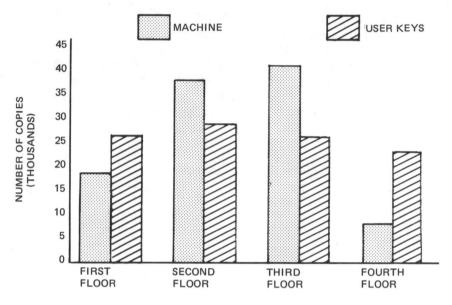

Figure 17   Comparison of Average Monthly Use of Machines and User Keys

On occasion, line graphs are used to compare things on different bases over the same period (see Figure 19).

There are two types of line graphs; those that show a time series and those that show interaction between two varying phenomena that is essentially a cause-effect relationship. In the time series, such as a month-by-month plot of sales, although the increment of time selected makes the sales levels in one sense dependent on time, the dependency

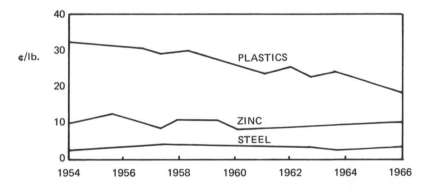

Figure 18   Average Price of Plastics, Zinc, and Steel, 1954-1968

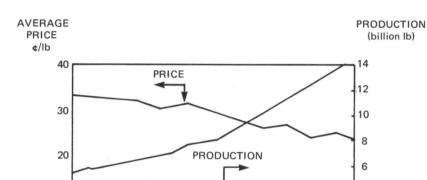

Figure 19   Production vs. Average Price of Plastics, 1954-1966

is not a cause-effect relationship. The month does not cause the sales; it merely reflects experience. Although seasonal patterns may become evident over extended time periods, time-series graphs indicate trends rather than interactions. In the more technical or scientific graphs, however, in which, for example, temperature is plotted against pressure, a cause-effect relationship is established in a mathematically reliable series of data.

The important point is that in a time-series graph, even though the line graph is continuous, the relationship is accurate only at selected points on the curve. Between the points connected by the line, the relationship between units of production and time, for example, is not functional.

CONSTRUCTION

Graphical illustrations and tables should be largely self-explanatory. To denote what they are designed to show, they should contain a title. For easy reference, they should be assigned a number.

Graphs should spell out the units of measurement. If several things are being compared, each should be clearly identified by a label or a legend. Sources should be credited.

Multiple line graphs should not contain so many comparisons that the lines become indistinct at converging points or that numerous criss-crossings create a bewildering maze. A graph such as the one in Figure

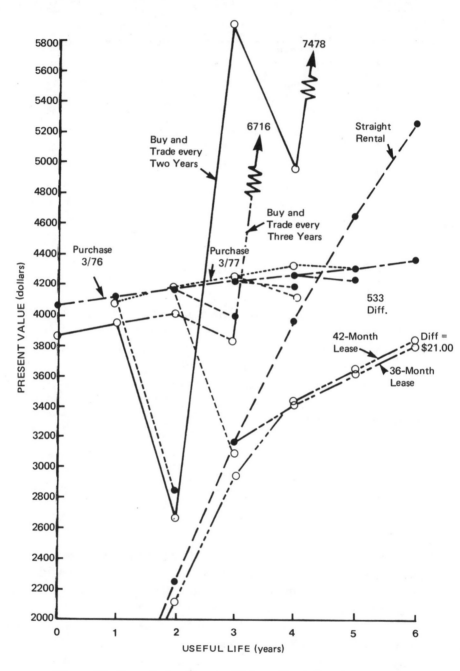

Figure 20 Cumulative Current Values: Rent, Purchase, or Lease

20 destroys the visual simplicity designed to aid easy comprehension.

Since the line graph is designed to help the reader visualize patterns of change or trends, it is important neither to suppress nor to exaggerate fluctuations by careless construction. Careless use of logarithmic scales, for example, can create distortions. Similarly, if one of the scales is altered, the comparison is distorted and the effect is misleading. Note in Figures 21 and 22, that altering the scale of the abscissa suggests that sales increased more dramatically than production, whereas they actually did not.

Tables, too, should specify categories, column headings, and units of measurement. If the same unit of measurement is used throughout, it can be spelled out in parentheses under the title; if the bases of measurement vary, the unit of measurement should be specified next to each item, as in Table 5.

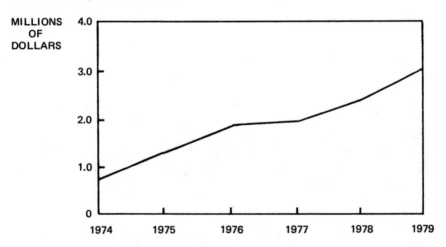

Figure 21 Company A's Sales

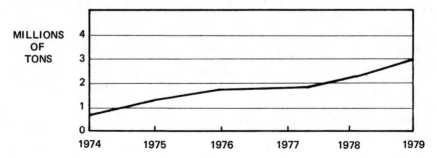

Figure 22   Company A's Production

Table 5 Sales Comparison

	1971	1972	1973	1974	1975	1976
Standard Corp. vs. Sensitive Devices, Inc.						
Standard Corp.						
Sales ($MM)	4.8	5.7	6.1	4.3*	6.2	8.8
Market Share (%)	51	53	55	45	55	60
Sensitive Devices						
Sales ($MM)	4.6	5.0	4.9	5.3	5.1	5.9
Market Share (%)	49	47	45	55	45	40

*Drop in sales due to loss of Newark plant by fire in 1959.

Many tables create problems not because of the complexity of the material, but because of the carelessness of the construction. Consider the poor reader faced with the task of following the analysis in Table 6.

Table 6 Cost Estimate, New Plastics Plant

	½ year 170,000 lb 73¢ lb	1 year 454,000 lb 73¢ lb	1½ years 1,000,000 lb/yr 73¢ lb	2 years 1,500,000 lb 73¢ lb
Annual Sales				
Rate	$123,000	$358,000	$730,000	$1,095,000
Material	77,000 (45¢ lb)	182,000 (40¢ lb)	400,000	600,000
Labor	27,000	47,000	100,000	150,000
GROSS PROFIT	19,000	129,000	230,000	345,000
Factory Overhead	82,500	82,500	82,500	82,500
R & D	12,000	12,000	20,000	30,000
Administration	51,000	51,000	51,000	51,000
Sales	30,500	30,500	35,500	40,000
Total	280,000	405,000	689,000	953,500
Net Cash Flow	-157,000	- 47,000	41,000	141,500
Depreciation	33,000	36,000	40,000	50,000
Total Loss	-$190,000	-$ 83,000	+$ 1,000	+$ 91,500

With a little thought, the writer could have saved the reader considerable time and trouble by presenting the information as in Table 7.

Table 7 Two-Year Profit Projection, New Plastics Plant

End of—	6 Mos.	12 Mos.	18 Mos.	24 Mos.
Annual Production—	170,000 lb.	454,000 lb	1,000,000 lb	1,500,000 lb
Selling Price—	73¢/lb	73¢/lb	73¢/lb	73¢/lb
Projected Sales	$123,000	$358,000	$730,000	$1,095,000
Less:				
Material Cost*	77,000	182,000	400,000	600,000
Labor Cost	27,000	47,000	100,000	150,000
Factory Overhead	82,500	82,500	82,500	82,500
R & D	12,000	12,000	20,000	30,000
Administration	51,000	51,000	51,000	51,000
Sales Expense	30,500	30,500	35,500	40,000
Total Operating Cost	280,000	405,000	689,000	953,500
Net Cash Flow	(157,000)	(47,000)	41,000	141,500
Less Depreciation	(33,000)	(36,000)	(40,000)	(50,000)
Profit (Loss)	($190,000)	($ 83,000)	$ 1,000	$ 91,500

* 45¢/lb first 6 months; 40¢/lb thereafter.

Finally, remember that a table is designed to provide concise elaboration of a topic thought. In discussing the table, therefore, confine your comments to facts not immediately evident (the validity of the data, assumptions on which it is based, and the method of derivation) and to the principal point(s) to be drawn. Do not let your commentary degenerate into a redundant recital of what is evident in the table. Although you may feel you are providing an exhaustive discussion, the reader may find it more exhausting than exhaustive.

Appendix I
Conventions

AGREEMENT

Use a Singular Verb When:

1. The subject is singular.

   Example: The <u>list</u> of contributors <u>was published</u> on Friday.

   Example: The <u>composition</u> of the limestone and clay deposits in both the Lewisburg and Blue Hills regions <u>is</u> suitable for use in the manufacture of cement.

2. A singular subject is linked to another noun or pronoun by a preposition.

   Example: The <u>instructor</u> as well as the students <u>is</u> anxious to begin work on the project.

   Example: An <u>officer</u> of the parent company, together with officers from all of the subsidiaries, <u>is attending</u> the meeting.

3. The subject is an indefinite pronoun such as *each, none, everyone,* and *anyone.*

   Example: <u>Each</u> of the clerks <u>was asked</u> for an opinion.

   Example: <u>None</u> of the tests <u>has been corrected</u>.

4. The subject is a collective noun.

   Example: A <u>series</u> of articles on drug abuse <u>is being prepared</u>.

   Example: The <u>board</u> <u>meets</u> once each month.

5. The subject is a quantity considered as a single unit.

   Example: <u>Two</u> <u>pints</u> <u>equals</u> one quart.

   Example: <u>Twenty-five</u> <u>milligrams</u> of some medications <u>is</u> more potent than one-hundred milligrams of others.

6. A fraction is followed by a singular noun.

   Example: <u>Four-fifths</u> of the <u>report</u> <u>is</u> complete.

   Example: <u>Ninety</u> <u>percent</u> of the <u>building</u> <u>is damaged</u>.

129

7. A relative pronoun refers to a singular noun or pronoun.

Example: Anyone who donates blood should not have a cold.

Example: She is the author of a book that has gone through six editions.

8. Both nouns used with correlatives are singular.

Example: Either snow or rain is expected.

Example: Not only John but also his wife earns more than $25,000 per year.

9. Only the second noun used with correlatives is singular.

Example: Neither the students nor the professor likes the arrangement.

Example: Not only the authors but also the editor was invited to the conference.

Use a Plural Verb When:

1. A plural noun or pronoun is used as the simple subject.

Example: Sales offices are located throughout the country.

Example: Those in upper levels of management rely on reports to keep informed.

2. A compound subject is used.

Example: Challenge and opportunity are important considerations in any job.

3. A group is considered as individuals.

Example: The board hold positions of importance in industry, government, and education.

Example: A number of employees believe they are underpaid.

4. A quantity is considered distributively.

Example: Three hundred acres were parcelled out.

5. A fraction is followed by a plural noun.

Example: Two-thirds of the employees agree with the policy.

Example: Twenty percent of the 1978 model cars were recalled for inspection.

6. A relative pronoun refers to a plural noun or pronoun.

Example: He is one of the executives who have been selected to attend an advanced program.

Example: <u>Those</u> <u>who</u> <u>want</u> to excel work hard.

7. Both nouns used with correlatives are plural.

Example: Neither the advantages nor the disadvantages were considered.

Example: Not only salaries but also fringe benefits were evaluated.

8. Only the second noun used with correlatives is plural.

Example: Not only the land but also the buildings are meticulously maintained.

Example: Neither the president of the university nor the trustees want to increase the tuition.

PUNCTUATION
The Comma Is Used To:

1. Separate elements in a series.

He edits reports, proposals, and manuals.

Arrogant men disdain outlines, lazy men admire them, and wise men use them.

2. Set off parenthetical expressions.

It is not, however, an ideal environment.

Most, if not all, large payrolls are prepared by a computer.

3. Separate introductory phrases or clauses.

Having completed the first phase, he concentrated on the second.

If you are not satisfied with an employee's performance, let him know.

4. Set off nonrestrictive clauses and phrases.

The Sandusky River, which flows through Ohio, empties into Lake Erie.

The George Washington Bridge, linking New York and New Jersey, spans the Hudson River.

5. Set off appositional elements.

Mr. Philbrick, the chief executive officer, will retire in June.

6. Indicate the omission of a verb.

Our writers prepare the first draft; our editors, the second.

7. Set off contrasting expressions.

He was valuable, not as a decision maker, but as a planner.

8. Set off inverted modifiers.

   The brochure, superbly written and exquisitely designed, is the paragon of good taste.

9. With balanced constructions using *the more . . . the larger . . . the greater.*

   The more responsible the position, the higher the salary.

The Semicolon Is Used:

1. To separate coordinate parts of a sentence that contain commas.

   The Big Three in the United States automotive industry are General Motors, which manufactures Chevrolets, Buicks, Pontiacs, Oldsmobiles, and Cadillacs; Ford, which manufactures Fords, Mercurys, and Lincolns; and Chrysler, which manufactures Plymouths, Dodges, and Chryslers.

2. Between clauses in a compound sentence when a conjunction is not used.

   An ammeter measures current; an ohmmeter, resistance.

3. Before expressions such as *namely, for example,* and *that is* when they introduce additional explanation.

   Course and coarse are homonyms; that is, words that sound the same but have different meanings.

4. Before conjunctive adverbs such as *therefore* and *thus.*

   The present procedure has created chaos; therefore, a new one is being developed.

The Colon Is Used:

1. After the salutation of a business letter.

   Dear Mr. Kane:

2. To introduce a series.

   Today's drug store sells a variety of things: prescriptive medicine, candy, stationery, liquor, cosmetics, and toys.

3. To separate clauses when the second explains the analogy suggested in the first.

   Writing a report is like custom-tailoring a suit: the user influences the style.

4. To introduce a long or formal quotation.

Samuel Johnson wrote: "I would rather be attacked than unnoticed. For the worst thing you can do to an author is to be silent as to his works."

The Dash Is Used:

1. To call attention to an aside.

Columbus believed—rightly, as we know now—that the earth is round.

2. Before a word that sums up a preceding series.

Fishing, camping, swimming—all kinds of outdoor activity interest tourists.

3. To set off words in apposition, amplification, or contrast.

We must keep in mind our principal objective—to create an environment in which people can prosper and pursue the ideals that made this country great.

The Hyphen Is Used With:

1. Compound nouns.

foot-candle, kilovolt-ampere, gram-calorie, man-hour

2. Compound adjectives.

10-yard run, high-speed equipment, two-story house, high-and low-pressure hoses

3. Fractions used as modifiers.

one-third share, three-fifths interest

4. Abbreviations of hyphenated terms.

a-c circuit, ft-lb

5. Prefixes to distinguish separate sounds.

re-enforce, co-axial

The Apostrophe Is Used To:

1. Signify possession.

company's profit, department's responsiveness

2. Denote a contraction.

it's, can't

3. Form the plural of letters and numerals.

c's, 8's

Quotation Marks Are Used To:

1. Enclose a direct quotation.

   Santayana said: "Fanaticism consists of redoubling your effort when you have forgotten your aim."

2. Indicate a title of an article in a magazine, newspaper, or trade journal.

   "Infrared Technology" was published in *Engineering News* last month.

Parentheses Are Used To Enclose:

1. Numbers or letters in an enumeration.

   Report writing involves: (1) collecting and analyzing data, (2) organizing material, (3) preparing a draft, and (4) review and revision.

2. Additional detail.

   In 1975, L.J. Ballard Company (now known as the Ballard Corporation) employed 800 people.

   Several large cities (e.g., San Francisco and Chicago) have benefitted from urban renewal projects.

3. Elements in an equation.

$$\frac{(X - 2)}{(Y + 1)} = Z$$

$$(1 + s - t) - (3x - 2) = 15$$

4. References.

   Schimler et al. [6] reported that . . .

   Production has increased steadily. (See Table 11.)

5. Identification of equations.

$$A + v = \frac{1 + s}{N_t} \qquad (14)$$

Brackets Are Used:

1. To show where editorial comment or correction has been inserted in quoted material.

   "It should be pointed out that this section [western Tennessee] has a suitable limestone deposit."

"When he was 34 [actually, he was 43], Mr. Evans was elected to the board."

2. With *sic* to denote that an error in the original material has been quoted exactly.

"In Lowell, Massachusets [*sic*] . . . ."

CAPITALIZATION

Points of the Compass Are Not Capitalized When:

1. Used to indicate directions.

New Hampshire is north of Massachusetts and east of Vermont.

2. Used in adjectival forms such as northern and eastern.

western Connecticut

a midwestern state

eastern Canada

Points of the Compass Are Capitalized When:

1. Used to identify a specific area.

Chicago's South Side

Southeast Asia

the Midwest

the Northern Hemisphere

Eastern-bloc countries

East Coast

2. Used to identify names of USDA districts.

West North Central area

Other Capitalization Rules:

1. Capitalize *government* only when it is used with a proper adjective.

U.S. Government

British Government

federal government

state government

2. Do not capitalize titles such as president, vice-president, and treasurer unless you are referring to individuals of unusual prominence.

the president of the company

The Vice-President of the United States

3. Similarly, do not capitalize words such as company and department unless they are part of a proper name.

Digital Equipment Corporation

CBI Publishing Company

Wang Laboratories

Personnel Department

Bessemer Division

a large company

an efficient department

the chemistry laboratory

4. Proprietary words should be capitalized.

Teflon

Monel

Mylar

Dry Ice

Fiberglas

Pyrex

NUMBERS

As a general rule, in textual discussion spell out all numbers through nine; use figures beginning with 10.

In tables, use a comma with numbers of four digits or more; in text, use a comma with numbers of five digits or more.

In text, very large numbers that might be subject to typographical error may be written: *2 million copies, $56 million.* Do not, however, write, for example, *11 thousand.*

When two numbers come together, spell out the first for clarity (e.g., twelve 16-inch guns, two 3-stage rockets).

In using statistics in other than table form, use figures for uniformity; for example, *The farmer shot 23 quail, 16 sheep, and 2 traveling salesmen.*

ABBREVIATIONS

Units	Abbr.	Units	Abbr.
ampere	amp	microampere	μa
barrel	bbl	microfarad	μa
British thermal unit	Btu	micron	μ
calorie	cal	miles per hour	mph
candlepower	cp	milliampere	ma
centimeter	cm	milligram	mg
cubic feet per hour	cfh	milliliter	ml
cubic feet per minute	cfm	millimeter	mm
cubic feet per second	cfs	million electron volts	Mev
cycle	(spell out)	millisecond	ms
cycles per second	cps	millivolt	mv
decibel	db	minute (time and angu-	
degree (angular)	deg	lar)	min
degree centigrade		month	mo
(Celsius)	C	ohm	(spell out)
degree Fahrenheit	F	ounce	oz
degree Kelvin	K	parts per million	ppm
feet per second	fps	pint	pt
feet per second per		pound (pounds)	lb
second	fps/sec^2	pounds per cubic	
foot	ft	foot(density)	pcf
foot-pound	ft-lb	pounds per square inch	psi
gallon	gal	(absolute pressure)	psia
gallons per day	gpd	(gage pressure)	psig
gallons per minute	gpm	quart	qt
gram	gm	revolutions per minute	rpm
hertz	Hz	roentgen	r
horsepower	hp	roentgen-equivalent-	
hour	hr	man	rem
hundredweight	cwt	roentgen-equivalent-	
inch	in.	physical	rep
kilohertz	kHz	second (time and angu-	
kilogram	kg	lar)	sec
kilometer	km	standard cubic foot	SCF
kilovolt	kv	standard cubic feet per	
kilovolt-ampere	kva	minute	SCFM
kilowatt	KW	thousand cubic feet	MCF
megohm	meg	ton	(spell out)
meter	m	volt	v
mho	(spell out)	week	wk

General Words	Abbr.	General Words	Abbr.
average	avg.	logarithm (base e)	ln
cathode-ray tube	CRT	liquefied natural gas	LNG
cost, insurance, and		liquefied petroleum gas	LPG
freight	c.i.f.	not available	n.a.
cost plus fixed fee	CPFF	not elsewhere classified	NEC
electromotive force	emf	original equipment	
free on board	f.o.b.	manufacturer	OEM
gross national product	GNP	outside diameter	OD
gross sales and admin.	GS&A	relative humidity	RH
infrared	IR	root mean square	rms
inside diameter	ID	Ultrahigh frequency	UHF
intermediate frequency	IF	versus	vs.
logarithm (base 10)	log	volt	v
		week	wk

A note of caution: If you decide to use abbreviations that may be confusing to the reader, spell out the complete term first and identify the abbreviation in parentheses before using it by itself; for example:

Characters per second (cps), so as not to mislead the reader into assuming cycles per second, for which cps is more commonly used. To avoid the difficulty in this instance, of course, you could substitute Baud rate (10x characters per second).

REFERENCES AND BIBLIOGRAPHY

If you do not wish to include a bibliography in your report, then refer to books, magazines, and journals in footnotes. In the first reference, give the complete citation and the specific pages referred to. If you refer to the same source thereafter, use the short version. If, however, you refer to it with no other reference intervening, you may simply use *ibid.* followed by the page(s) cited. Thus,

First Reference:
> Clarence B. Nickerson, *Accounting Handbook For Nonaccountants,* 2nd ed., Boston, Mass.: CBI Publishing Company, Inc., 1979, pp. 579–580.

No Reference Intervening:
> *Ibid.,* p. 472.

Intervening Reference:
> Stanford L. Optner, *Systems Analysis for Business Management,* Englewood Cliffs, N.J., Prentice-Hall, Inc., 1960, p. 6.

Short Reference:
Nickerson, *Accounting Handbook for Nonaccountants,* p. 472.

A bibliography differs from a list of references in that the works listed in a bibliography are not necessarily referred to in the text. A bibliography is arranged alphabetically by author. A reference list, however, need not be arranged alphabetically; instead, it may appear in the sequence in which each publication is cited.

In some instances, the author may choose to provide a bibliography and also to reference some or all of the publications. In that event, textual references do not appear in chronological sequence; instead, they are related to the sequence in which the publication appears in the bibliography.

Although the form in which various publications are listed may vary slightly from publication to publication, the following forms are commonly used in bibliographies.

Books

Anastasi, Thomas E., Jr., *Communicating for Results*, Menlo Park, Calif.: Cummings Publishing Company, Inc., 1972.

Rose, Arthur, and Rose, Elizabeth, eds., *The Condensed Chemical Dictionary*, 7th ed., New York: Reinhold Publishing Corporation, 1966.

Magazine Articles, Author Known

Tillman, John, "How High The Moon," *Science and Technology,* Vol. 35, June 1960, pp. 99-100.

Magazine Articles, Author Unknown

"Women in the Armed Forces," *Newsweek,* February 18, 1980, pp. 34-41.

Journal Articles

Argo, W. B., and Smith, J. M., Chem. Eng. Prog., 49, 443 (1953).

Fischler, H.; Frei, E. H.; Spira, D.; and Rubenstein, M., "Dynamic Response of Middle-Ear Structures," *J. Acoust. Soc. Am.* XLI, No. 5 (1967), pp. 1220-31.

Reports, Author(s) Known

George, James H. H.; Stratton, Lawrence; and Acton, Richard G.,

Prospects for Electric Vehicles, Cambridge, Mass.: Arthur D. Little, Inc., May 15, 1968.

Reports, Author(s) Unknown

Arthur D. Little, Inc., *Automobile Market Dynamics,* Cambridge, Mass., February 1976.

Thesis

Massa, J. L., *Theoretical and Experimental Studies of Ionization Exchange between the Ionosphere and Plasmasphere,* Ph.D. Thesis, Ann Arbor, Mich.: University of Michigan, 1974.

Papers

Teller, Edward, "Water Generation in Space," Conference on *Nutrition in Space and Related Waste Problems,* NASA Special Publication #70, Washington, D.C.: U.S. Government Printing Office, 1964.

Margolin, S., and Cooper, C., "Environmental Impact Assessment—The Two-Minute Mile," paper presented at 72nd Annual Meeting of the American Institute of Chemical Engineers, San Francisco, Calif., November 1979.

Newspaper Articles

"3 Mile Isle: New Trouble," *Boston Herald American,* February 14, 1980, p. C10.

"So Who Won—" (Editorial): *The Sun* (Lowell, Mass.), February 12, 1980, p. 6.

Appendix II
Answers to
Exercises

CHAPTER 2 ORGANIZATION: FOCUS AND IMPACT

1. c,d,g,j

2. A theme is stated in a complete sentence. It serves as the focus of the report. It is usually the conclusion or recommendation.

3. One way of presenting the information is as follows:

SUMMARY

Purpose and Scope

During the 1978-79 season, our Metropole operation incurred an operating loss of $11,900, compared with a planned profit of $93,200. Management therefore asked that the operation be reviewed to determine the principal factors that contributed to the deficit, and to recommend corrective action.

The study was based on an analysis of financial controls, security, reporting procedures, staffing policy, and the lease agreement.

Conclusion

Metropole operated at a loss during the 1978-79 season because:

1. Inadequate controls and security resulted in food and beverage costs 10 percent higher than planned;

2. Sales were reported inaccurately;

3. Metropole's remote location resulted in serious labor shortages; and

4. According to the lease agreement, we are responsible for cleaning all food-service areas, but the operating plan made no provision for this cost, which represented $18,800, or 2.1 percent of sales.

Recommendations

1. Tighten security and financial controls.
2. Change the format for reporting sales.
3. Arrange for additional housing for employees.
4. Make certain that allocated expenses reflect leasing arrangements.

   I. Highlights of Performance vs. Plan
      A. Variances
      B. Validity of Projections
   II. Operating Procedures
      A. Financial Controls
         1. Current Practice
         2. Recommended Change
      B. Security
         1. Current Practice
         2. Recommended Changes
      C. Reporting Methods
         1. Current Practice
         2. Recommended Changes
   III. Lease Analysis
      A. Terms
      B. Effect on Performance
      C. Suggested Revisions

---

4. The report should stress that the purpose is to determine whether there is a market for Bigelow's high-purity generator. The basis for the determination—and hence, the scope—is the size of the present and future markets and the market share it could hope to gain in four industrial sectors: semiconductor, pharmaceutical, food processing, and specialty gases. The ancillary considerations such as consistency of supply, reaction of existing suppliers, benefits of on-site generation, and price advantages should be considered as part of the analysis of the markets.

The conclusions should state whether there is or is not a market in each of the four industrial sectors, and the reasons supporting the conclusions should be based on the size of the present and future markets and the expected market share.

The data contained under "Conclusions" in the original report is at best a series of factors that may be considered to determine the size of the markets, but in the form presented it is not related clearly to the markets under study. Much of the material belongs more appropriately in sections of the body of the report, where the detailed discussion takes place.

5. Suggested revision to memo.

As you requested, I have looked into the operation of the security vault to: (1) identify problems and (2) suggest corrective measures.

The problems are directly attributable to a shortage of qualified people. First, we are short two workers: Arthur Jones, who retired on January 31, and John Doe, who left the bank on March 11. Second, we need two additional people to satisfy management's directive that we improve the dual-control system of our Collateral Vault. Finally, some of our present staff are not qualified for these jobs; they should be replaced.

Since it is patently impractical to make all of the required changes at one time, I propose a two-step approach. First, we should replace Jones and Doe and hire the two additional people needed for dual control. Second, when these steps have been taken we can transfer other members of the department as replacements become available.

To ensure that we get the proper replacements, we should adopt the following guidelines. The replacements should be checked carefully (probably by our security officer), be intelligent enough to understand their duties, and be responsible enough to handle securities worth billions of dollars. They should not be people with health problems or people "who haven't made it" in other departments. Neither should they be agency personnel, students on summer vacation, nor (except for a few selected retirees) part-time workers.

I have specific recommendations about the present staff, but because of the obvious need for confidentiality, I would prefer to discuss them privately with you, one of your staff, or the Personnel Department.

CHAPTER 3   OUTLINING: BUILDING THE FRAMEWORK

1. According to the main theme, or conclusion, the expansion of the NHL, including the merger with the WHA, has depleted the supply of talent and created greater bargaining power for the players. The outline, however, includes a history of expansion but no detail in support of the depletion of talent and greater bargaining power of players.

2. Glass containers

I. Common Types
   Drinking Glasses
   Bottles
   Aquarium Tanks
II. Design Criteria
   Convenience
   Usefulness
   Economy
III. Production Considerations
   Equipment
   Labor
   Cost

IV. Sales Outlets
   Department Stores
   Novelty Stores
   Discount Stores
   Pet Shops
V. Promotion
   Newspaper Ads
   Circulars
   Radio Commercials

3. I. Economic Indicators
   Population
   1,6
   Employment
   10,4,13
   Personal Income
   8

II. Student Characteristics
   9,14,3,5,12,15,18,16
III. Location of College
   2,7,11,17

4. Your own summary and outline.

CHAPTER 5   ORDERLY DEVELOPMENT: THE PARAGRAPH PRINCIPLE

1. a. The topic sentence suggests a multitude of problems. One problem is mentioned. The last sentence is not related to the others.

   b. The paragraph does not explain the potential problems of playing devil's advocate. The sequence of sentences is poor. The first sentence and half of the second should be combined. The last sentence should come second. The third sentence should remain third, but further elaboration should follow.

    c. A second thought is introduced beginning with "In order to control. . . ." Still a third thought is contained in the combination of the last two sentences.

    d. The two points mentioned in the topic (first) sentence are not evenly developed. The second point is at best hinted at in the development, while the first point receives most of the attention.

    e. Good development. Topic idea is in the first sentence. The remaining sentences support it.

    f. The topic sentence is again left undeveloped, while new thoughts are introduced in the second and third sentences.

2. a. poor

   b. good

   c. marginal

   d. good

   e. poor

   f. marginal

   g. poor

   h. marginal

3. Sequence is 5-2-7-6-3-1-4.

4. Sequence is 4-9-8-1-6-3.

   Sentences 2-5-7-10 do not belong in the paragraph.

5. A single sentence incorporating the two problems should stand as a one-sentence paragraph. Separate paragraphs should then be devoted to each point. Finally, one paragraph should discuss whether these two problems will be overcome. Thus,

---

    Two temporary but substantial impediments stand in the way of successful adoption of automated composition systems by in-plant publishing activities: (1) the wide diversity of products, while contributing to a rapid evolution of systems, has also caused confusion in the market; and (2) new systems call for new skills, new organizations, and new management practices.

    The confusion in the market has been enhanced by product incompatibility and competitive pressure. Each supplier promulgates its own standards. Thus, phototypesetters all use different codes, copy-processing systems call for complex and often special interfaces, and editing terminals are designed to operate only with other systems of the same manufacturer. The one exception is the teletypesetter (TTS) code, which has survived despite its inefficiency, because it is the lowest common denominator. Under competitive pressures, suppliers have added to the confusion by announcing products before they have been tested, sometimes before they have been built, and nearly always long before they have become available for shipment. Buyers have become frequently confused because suppliers have offered surprisingly little technical information.

For most users, the organization and management of automated composition has been a difficult issue to resolve. Installations have suffered from the parochial interests of the production department or from the more experimental, often hardware-oriented attitude of the data processing department.

We are, nonetheless, optimistic that these problems will gradually be overcome. Over the short term, the confusion in the market will diminish because there will be fewer suppliers. Over the long term, equipment acquired during the current stage of confusion and performing at only marginal levels will have to be substantially modified or replaced. In the organization and management of these systems, changes are already emerging. The reaction of trade compositors, for example, has gradually changed from resistance to genuine interest. Some new organization patterns have emerged already, and others will. "Assistant Managing Editor for Production," for example, identifies the newsroom systems manager at a major newspaper; "Vice-President for Communications" (or "for Information Systems") is a corporate assignment that increasingly encompasses automated composition and business information systems along with other responsibilities, including data processing, library functions, public relations, and word processing.

In the light of these encouraging signs, therefore, we believe that the growth of automated systems over the long term will not be hampered by these problems, and that advancing technology will satisfy the needs of a wide variety of users.

CHAPTER 6   EDITING THE DRAFT: APPLYING THE FINISH

1. Clarity

   a. Like me, he is doing extensive research on the nuclear genetics of invertebrates.

   b. Since his appointment as corporate counsel, Mr. Smith is responsible for handling all of the company's legal problems.

   c. Three classes of data were obtained: male and female income, commuting distances and times, and average hours worked.

   d. His assignment was to evaluate how relocating the international airport would affect residents of the surrounding area.

   e. In an airplane, we crossed in one day a region that took our grandparents two months to cross.

   f. Although the same number of banks submitted data for participation in the Functional Cost Program in both 1978 and 1979, the percentage of participants was higher in 1979 because of a decrease in overall membership.

   g. I hope you received from the state police the road information you need for your emergency trip.

   h. As I was backing out of my driveway, I collided with a car. On several other occasions, the same kind of accident resulted under similar circumstances.

   i. Your company should not use unique formats in government reports unless the government approves.

   j. When a colleague tried to offer advice, the new employee's anger was neither tactful nor appropriate.

2. Conciseness

   a. The manpower forecast bases projected needs on historical use patterns.

   b. The company can develop an energy resource base efficiently only if it keeps abreast of the state of the art.

   c. The proposed airport will create a noise problem.

   d. Experiments with mice proved that smoking causes forms of cancer.

   e. A significantly larger number of checking accounts are maintained in banks that do not require a minimum balance.

f. The department's margin in 1979 was approximately 10 percent of sales.

g. Because of today's volatile economic and social environment, planning and decision making for a college must be based on comprehensive data.

h. The research team interviewed leading citizens to determine whether the new post office should be built near the Pine Bluffs shopping center.

i. The annual meeting of the Credit Union will be held in the auditorium on January 27 at 10 A.M.

j. The company needs a broader product line.

k. The company's three divisions occupy separate buildings.

l. The average salary for secretaries in this area is $12,000 per year.

m. At least 100 names were added to the list.

n. To reduce cost and speed delivery, postmarking in each intermediate post office was eliminated a number of years ago.

o. He reorganized the department.

3. An audience needs three pieces of information about a presentation: the reason for it, the central idea, and the scope. To develop perspective and place the purpose in context, general background information may be needed at the outset. The scope defines the major areas you intend to discuss in support of the central idea. By providing focus and direction, the central idea and the scope thus help the audience to better understand the details provided in the body of the presentation.

4. Revised Memo

To: Entire Staff

From: Telephone Supervisor

Subject: Telephone Service

Recently, we have received a number of complaints from the staff about telephone service, especially service at the switchboard and lost calls. We understand your concerns and are working to correct the problems.

A major part of the problem is the heavy usage. On a typical day, our staff makes 16,000 calls (both inside and outside the company) and 4,300 calls come into the company. Since our system is more than 20 years old, this heavy use increases the number of malfunctions — everything from lights out on the telephone to call cut-offs. And, of course, the sheer number of calls has meant delays in operator response.

To correct these problems, we are taking both long- and short-term remedies. We expect to have a new telephone system on line within the next 8 to 12 months. In the meantime, we are expanding our present 160-line system. Last month, for example, we increased the capacity of the 555 - 1100 lines and dial 9-lines by 10 percent. We are also adding more operators.

Other problems, however, are beyond our control. The construction project at Tulip Plaza, for example, has interrupted our service periodically. Sometimes the problem lies at the other end of the line. In such cases, we can only report the problem to the Telephone Company.

Until our new system is installed and our operator staff is increased, you can help us by reporting all problems as quickly as possible. Call the Chief Operator on extension 500 or 501. She will log in the problem and either take action directly or refer it to the Telephone Company for action and follow through on it until it is remedied.

Thank you for your cooperation.